THE HOUSES
OF PARLIAMENT

A Guide to the Palace of Westminster

THE HOUSES
OF PARLIAMENT

A Guide to the Palace of Westminster

Sir Bryan H. Fell, K.C.M.G., C.B.
late Principal Clerk in the House of Commons

and

K. R. Mackenzie, C.B.
late Clerk of Public Bills in the House of Commons

Fifteenth edition revised by D. L. Natzler
A Deputy Principal Clerk

Published with the authority of the Lord Great Chamberlain,
the Lord Chancellor and the Speaker of the House of Commons

London: HMSO

Fifteenth edition 1994
First edition 1930

ISBN 0 11 701579 2

Front cover:
Big Ben illuminated at dusk. Joe Cornish/Tony Stone Worldwide.

Back cover:
Chariot horse, Boadicea's Monument, with Big Ben beyond. John Bethell.

Frontispiece:
The Houses of Parliament from Victoria Tower. Clive Friend/HMSO.

HMSO publications are available from:

HMSO Publications Centre
(Mail, fax and telephone orders only)
PO Box 276, London, SW8 5DT
Telephone orders 071-873 9090
General enquiries 071-873 0011
(queuing system in operation for both numbers)
Fax orders 071-873 8200

HMSO Bookshops
49 High Holborn, London, WC1V 6HB
(counter service only)
071-873 0011 Fax 071-873 8200
258 Broad Street, Birmingham, B1 2HE
021-643 3740 Fax 021-643 6510
33 Wine Street, Bristol, BS1 2BQ
0272 264306 Fax 0272 294515
9-21 Princess Street, Manchester, M60 8AS
061-834 7201 Fax 061-833 0634
16 Arthur Street, Belfast, BT1 4GD
0232 238451 Fax 0232 235401
71 Lothian Road, Edinburgh, EH3 9AZ
031-228 4181 Fax 031-229 2734

HMSO's Accredited Agents
(see Yellow Pages)

and through good booksellers

Printed in the United Kingdom for HMSO.
Dd. 293658, 1/94, C50, 3396/4, 5673, 238713.

Almighty God, by whom alone Kings reign and Princes decree justice, and from whom alone cometh all counsel, wisdom and understanding; we thine unworthy servants here gathered together in Thy Name, do most humbly beseech Thee to send down Thy Heavenly Wisdom from above, to direct and guide us in all our consultations: and grant that, we having Thy fear always before our eyes, and laying aside all private interests, prejudices and partial affections, the result of all our counsels may be to the glory of Thy blessed Name, the maintenance of true Religion and Justice, the safety, honour and happiness of the Queen, the publick wealth, peace and tranquillity of the Realm, and the uniting and knitting together of the hearts of all persons and estates within the same, in true Christian Love and Charity one towards another, through Jesus Christ our Lord and Saviour.

The Prayer used by both Houses of Parliament

Admission to the Palace of Westminster

Permits for guided parties to tour the principal rooms of the Palace of Westminster can be obtained by application to Members of either House. The Palace is closed to visitors on Saturdays, Sundays, Public Holidays and during the Christmas Recess.

Admission to Sittings of the House of Lords

A limited number of seats are available for members of the general public on Tuesdays and Wednesdays at 2.40 p.m., Thursdays at 3.10 p.m., frequently on Mondays at 2.40 p.m. and occasionally on Fridays at 11.10 a.m. Visitors wait outside St Stephen's Entrance until directed by the police to move into the Peers' Corridor. Members and Officers of either House may also apply to Black Rod's Office to obtain seats for visitors to attend sittings of the House of Lords. During the sitting of the House application must be made to the Doorkeeper at the Control Table in the Peers' Lobby.

Admission to Sittings of the House of Commons

On sitting days the Gallery is open to the public, who can, without applying to a Member of Parliament, obtain orders for the Strangers' Gallery after 4.15 p.m. (10 a.m. on Fridays), provided there is room. Orders for this Gallery are issued direct to applicants by the Admission Order Office in the Central Lobby, which is reached by St Stephen's Entrance, but at times a long wait may be necessary.

Application for orders of admission may be made in advance to a Member of Parliament. These orders admit the holder to the Gallery at 2.30 p.m. (9.30 a.m. on Fridays) without delay, if presented before 3 p.m. (10 a.m. on Fridays).

Commonwealth and foreign visitors who present an introduction from their High Commissioners or Embassies may apply for an order direct to the Admission Order Office.

Admission to House of Lords Record Office

Members of the public are admitted to the Search Room in order to consult the records of Parliament between 9.30 a.m. and 5 p.m., Mondays to Fridays. Applications should, if possible, be made by letter or by telephone (071–219 3074) at least 24 hours in advance.

Contents

THE HOUSE OF COMMONS

PARLIAMENT: ITS COMPOSITION, PROCEDURE AND CEREMONIAL

List of Illustrations

Acknowledgements

For their kindness in helping me to prepare this edition I am much indebted to many colleagues from the Palace of Westminster, and in particular to George Chowdharay-Best, Janric Craigavon, Malcolm Hay, Andy Makepeace, Andrew Makower, Hilary Natzler and Sandra Wedgwood. My thanks also to Bob Barnard of HMSO and to the Speaker's Art Fund.

The author and the publisher would like to thank the following for permission to reproduce illustrations: John Bethell, back cover; Joe Cornish/Tony Stone Worldwide, front cover; Clive Friend, frontispiece; Jim James/Press Association, no. 17; Jarrold Publishing, nos 5 and 12; Terry Moore, no. 13; Pitkin Pictorials Ltd, nos 3, 8, 9 and 18; Woodmansterne, no. 1. All other illustrations are Crown copyright.

1   Westminster Hall, looking south towards St Stephen's Porch

The Ancient
and Modern Palaces

The Palace of Westminster occupies the site of the old Royal Palace, which was the chief residence of the King from the time of Edward the Confessor to Henry VIII. The building was much damaged by fire in 1512, and Henry VIII acquired York Place, which he renamed Whitehall, from Cardinal Wolsey in 1529 and built St James's Palace in 1532. The old palace then ceased to be a royal residence but has remained a royal palace, and as such was under the charge of the Lord Great Chamberlain, a hereditary officer of state, until 1965. Since then his jurisdiction in the palace has been confined to the Queen's Robing Room, the staircase and ante-room thereto adjoining, and the Royal Gallery. Control of the parts of the building occupied by the Lords and the Commons has been vested respectively in the Lord Chancellor and Mr Speaker. Control of Westminster Hall and the Crypt Chapel is shared between the Lord Great Chamberlain, the Lord Chancellor and Mr Speaker. Since 1992, the Parliamentary Works Directorate, under the authority of both Houses, has been responsible for the fabric of the Palace and the provision of furnishing, fuel and light.

Westminster Hall

Westminster Hall is the oldest remaining part of the Palace, and its walls incorporate part at least of the walls of the original Hall built by William Rufus between 1097 and 1099. Several arches from the original Norman arcade which ran the length of the Hall above the string course have survived, beside the present windows; they are now concealed behind hinged wooden panels. Rufus called Westminster Hall the New Hall to distinguish it from the Great Hall of the Confessor's Palace which lay to the south. It is for this reason that the yard in front of the north end is known as New Palace Yard. The Hall was an aisled building, its roof supported on two rows of columns, probably of wood.

The Hall which we now see was given its present character as a result of the rebuilding by Richard II between 1394 and 1399; his badge, a chained hart, is repeated along the string course. The architect was Henry Yevele, the first great exponent of the Perpendicular style, much of whose work survives in Westminster Abbey. Geoffrey Chaucer, the poet, was Clerk of the Works at the Palace of Westminster from 1389 to 1391. The internal length of the Hall is about 240 ft (73.1 m) the breadth about 68 ft (20.7 m), and the height to the centre apex about 92 ft (28 m). It is thus one of the largest ancient buildings in Europe undivided by columns, being some 20 ft (6 m) shorter and narrower than the Palazzo della Ragione at Padua, built about the same time.

The hammer-beam roof has been described as 'quite without a rival in any part of the world, not only for the ingenuity of its construction, but on account of the perfection and delicacy of its details'. It is the work of Hugh Herland who became Edward III's master carpenter in 1375 and designed the canopy for his tomb in Westminster Abbey. Oak for the original roof was brought from the royal woods at Odiham and Aliceholt in Hampshire, from Stoke D'Abernon in Surrey, and from a park near Northaw in Hertfordshire. The timber was prepared at Farnham and taken by road to Ham near Chertsey, whence it was carried to Westminster by water.

The angels at the ends of the hammer-beams were carved by Robert Grassington. The statues of the six kings on the south wall were carved by Thomas Canon in 1394–98; originally painted by Nicholas Tryer, traces of colour have recently been rediscovered and conserved. The five larger statues of kings on the sills of windows in the east wall are of the same period and were originally on the north front of the Hall.

In the years 1819–20 the entrance front was restored in Bath stone and the roof was repaired with forty loads of well-seasoned oak from old ships broken up in Portsmouth dockyard. Owing to the ravages of the death-watch beetle, a further repair of the roof had to be undertaken between 1914 and 1923 under the supervision of Sir Frank Baines. The whole of the roof was strengthened by concealed steel work, and the decayed portions were replaced with new oak from the estate of Lord Courthope, near Wadhurst, East Sussex. During these repairs some tennis balls, believed to be of the time of Henry VIII, were found in the roof. The delicate tracery of the timbers of the roof is now shown in full detail by the special roof lighting which was presented by the Inter-Parliamentary Union on the occasion of their meeting in the Hall in 1975. In 1822 the lantern, which had been glazed in 1663, was rebuilt by Soane on more slender lines. Part of the lantern and a considerable area of the roof boarding and rafters were destroyed by fire in the air raid on 10 May 1941 (*see* p. 27); the oak for these repairs was again provided from the Wadhurst estate. The Hall was flooded in 1237, 1242, 1579, 1841, and, in spite of the making of the Thames embankment, again in 1928.

On 17 June 1974 a bomb exploded in the Grand Committee Room annexe adjoining the north-west corner of the Hall. The explosion wrecked part of the annexe, damaged two of the Hall's flying buttresses and blew out windows in the Hall, including the great window over the main entrance. It also started a fire which damaged part of the external stonework and roof of the hall; some of the timbers are still black from the fire. Archaeological investigations in the ruins of the annexe revealed that the site of the Hall (on what was then Thorney Island) had been inhabited from an early period.

St Stephen's Porch

The great window at the south end and the flight of steps leading up to it were built by Sir Charles Barry when he cut the archway in the old south wall, to create St Stephen's Porch.

The nineteenth-century window, which contained armorial bearings of the kings and queens of England, was destroyed in an air raid. The new window, by Sir Ninian Comper, contains the coats of arms or monograms of the Members and staff of both Houses who fell in the Second World War, and the badges of their regiment, squadron or ship. Below the window is a memorial by Bertram MacKennal to those from both Houses who were killed in the First World War. On the west wall hangs a painting of Moses receiving the Law on Mount Sinai, by Benjamin West, originally commissioned for Windsor Castle by George III, presented in 1946 by the Earl of Crawford and Balcarres to the Royal Courts of Justice and transferred to the Palace in 1958.

St Stephen's Entrance

St Stephen's Entrance is the main public entrance for those wishing to attend a sitting of either House. Inside are two mahogany panels painted by MacDonald Gill and fitted in 1932, one showing a map of London and the Underground Railway network, presented by the Underground Railway Company, and the other showing the plan of the present building superimposed on the old palace, presented by Lt. Col. Tebbutt.

Law Courts

Westminster Hall was the Great Hall of the Royal Palace, and as such it was from the earliest times the meeting-place of the King's Great Council, out of which grew both the Courts of Justice and Parliament. By the end of the thirteenth century the Courts of King's Bench, Common Pleas, Exchequer and Chancery were settled at Westminster. King's Bench and Chancery sat in the south-east and south-west corners of the Hall respectively and Common Pleas near the middle of the west wall. The Exchequer Court was outside the Hall in a building adjoining the northern end of the west wall.

In 1820–25 Sir John Soane built a range of buildings along the west side of the Hall, ingeniously placed between the buttresses and with doorways leading into the Hall. Here the Courts remained until 1882, when the Royal Courts of Justice were opened in the Strand. Soane's remaining buildings were demolished and partially replaced by J. L. Pearson. These rooms now house the offices of the United Kingdom branch of the Commonwealth Parliamentary Association and a number of meeting rooms.

In 1978 a newly refitted Conference Room was opened, and named the Jubilee Room in honour of H.M. The Queen's Silver Jubilee of 1977. Pearson also created the Grand Committee Room annexe at the north-west corner of the Hall. Here Cecil Rhodes and Dr Jameson were heard by a Select Committee of the House of Commons in 1897. It was completely refurbished in 1975, and is used on occasions for Select Committee hearings and public meetings. A stairlift providing access for disabled people was installed in 1992.

State Trials

Though it was the custom from the earliest times to proclaim Parliaments in the Great Hall, few are recorded as having met there. The ceremonial opening of Parliament appears normally to have taken place in the Painted Chamber before 1512, and in the old House of Lords chamber after 1536 (*see* p. 16). The Great Hall was, however, used for the extraordinary assemblies at which Edward II and Richard II were deposed. In addition to its use by the ordinary Courts of Law, Westminster Hall was the scene of most of the celebrated state trials and impeachments, including those of Sir William Wallace (1305), Perkin Warbeck (1498), Saint Thomas More and Saint John Fisher (1535), The Duke of Somerset, Protector (1551), Guy Fawkes (1606), The Earl of Strafford (1641), Charles I (1649), The Seven Bishops (1688), Dr Sacheverell (1710), The rebel lords of the '15 (1716), The rebel lords of the '45 (1746–7) and Warren Hastings (1788–95).

The last state trial held in the Hall was the impeachment of Henry Dundas, Viscount Melville, in 1806.

Banquets &c.

The Hall was also used for great state ceremonies and coronation feasts from Stephen to George IV. Until the coronation of James II the King came in procession by river from the Tower to Westminster Hall, where he was elevated in what was known as the Marble Chair before entering the Abbey Church. A banquet was then held in the Hall, and the King's Champion rode into the Hall in full armour to challenge anyone who disputed the King's right to succeed. The last banquet, accompanied by the challenge, was held at the coronation of George IV in 1821. At the coronations of George V, George VI and H.M. The Queen luncheons were served in the Hall for Members of both Houses of Parliament. The luncheon which was given in the Hall to representatives of Dominion Parliaments on the first occasion led to the formation of the Commonwealth Parliamentary Association. Here too Oliver Cromwell took the oath as Lord Protector in 1653, and in 1657, adorned in princely state, he took his seat in the Coronation Chair. In 1661 when his body was exhumed, the head was set up on a pole on the roof of the Hall and remained there till 1684.

As early as the reign of Edward III Flemish and native hucksters had their stalls in the Hall; in the sixteenth century the scholars of Westminster School obtained the right to erect stalls for the sale of their books; and Pepys often refers to the booksellers and haberdashers. These stalls and the coffee-houses outside the north door were swept away at the end of the eighteenth century.

Ceremonies

The Hall is still used for occasions of great state and parliamentary ceremony. Modern events, commemorated by tablets in the floor of the Hall, have included the lying-in-state of Mr Gladstone on 26–27 May 1898, and of King Edward VII on 17–19 May 1910; the presentation of Loyal Addresses to King George V by both Houses of Parliament on the occasion of his Silver Jubilee, 9 May 1935, and his lying-in-state, 23–28 January 1936; the lying-in-state of King George VI, 11–15 February 1952, of Queen Mary, 29–31 March 1953, and of Sir Winston Churchill, 27–29 January 1965; and the presentation of Loyal Addresses to H.M. The Queen by both Houses of Parliament on the occasions of her Silver Jubilee, 4 May 1977 and of the Tercentenary of the Revolutions of 1688–89, 20 July 1988. Here too lay the coffins of the forty-eight persons who were killed in the airship R 101 when it crashed near Beauvais in October 1930. Another tablet commemorates the presentation of Addresses to H.M. The Queen on 22 June 1965 to mark the seventh centenary of the Parliament to which Simon de Montfort, Earl of Leicester, caused to be summoned, for the first time, citizens and burgesses.

H.M. The Queen and H.R.H. Prince Philip attended the opening ceremonies of conferences of the Commonwealth Parliamentary Association (25 September 1961, 12 September 1973 and 25 September 1986), the Inter-Parliamentary Union (12 September 1957 and 4 September 1975), and the 10th anniversary congress of the North Atlantic Treaty Organization (5 June 1959). They also attended the celebration of the 25th anniversary of the signing of the Charter of the United Nations on 26 June 1970. The opening ceremonies of the 28th and 36th Annual Sessions of the North Atlantic Assembly were held in the Hall on 17 November 1982 and 28 November 1990 respectively.

On 26 October 1950, on the occasion of the opening of the new Commons Chamber, King George VI received Addresses from both

Houses of Parliament in the presence of the Speakers or presiding officers of twenty-eight Commonwealth legislatures. On 30 November 1954, on his eightieth birthday, Sir Winston Churchill was presented with his portrait by both Houses of Parliament and with an illuminated volume of Members' signatures by the Commons. The two Houses of Parliament received the President of France and Madame Lebrun on 23 March 1939; and on 7 April 1960 President de Gaulle addressed both Houses in French. On 26 May 1976, to mark the bicentenary of the United States of America, the Speaker of the House of Commons presented a golden copy of Magna Carta to the Speaker of the House of Representatives.

Access to St Stephen's Chapel

The tablet on the wall in the south-east corner marks the position of the doorway used from 1547 to 1680 as the principal means of access to the House of Commons, via the Cloisters and a flight of steps to the vestibule on the west front of St Stephen's Chapel. After 1680 a doorway cut through the centre of the south wall of Westminster Hall was used instead, to reach the west doors of St Stephen's Chapel.

St Stephen's Hall

St Stephen's Chapel

St Stephen's Hall stands on the site of the royal chapel of St Stephen, which along with the other free chapels was suppressed by a statute of Edward VI in 1547 and handed over by him to the Commons. The House of Commons sat here until the fire of 1834. Before 1547 the Commons had no meeting-place of their own and sat for the most part either in the Chapter House or the Refectory of Westminster Abbey.

The original Norman chapel traditionally ascribed to the reign of King Stephen was pulled down in 1292 by Edward I, who began rebuilding it as a two-storeyed building after the manner of St Louis's Sainte Chapelle in Paris, the upper chapel being St Stephen's, the lower the chapel of St Mary Undercroft (see p. 11). The building was finished in 1348 by Edward III, who founded the College of St Stephen, consisting of a dean and twelve canons. There can be no doubt that, in the words of John Carter,

7

the antiquarian, the chapel 'must have been the first of all the architectural works of the land'. The interior was richly decorated with sculpture, paintings and stained glass. The wall paintings were covered with wainscotting by Sir Christopher Wren in 1692, and in 1707 he reconstructed the chapel and built galleries to accommodate the Scottish Members. In 1800 it became necessary still further to 'stretch' the Chamber to make room for the Irish Members. The walls were cut away and the remains of the mural decorations destroyed. Some fragments survive in the British Museum; an idea of the beauty of some of the paintings may be gained from the reconstructions by Professor Tristram in the Lobby at the bottom of the Terrace stairs (*see* p. 61).

All the great events in English parliamentary history from the time of Edward VI to William IV took place in the chapel: it was here that the struggle for constitutional government was fought with the Stuarts by Eliot, Pym and Hampden; that Burke pleaded for an understanding of the American colonies; that Pitt and Fox contended on the questions of peace and war; that Wilberforce espoused the cause of the abolition of the slave trade and of slavery; and that the long contest for the Reform Bill was carried through. The present seating plan of the Commons, with Members facing each other in parallel rows like a choir in a chapel, can perhaps be traced back to the influence of the chapel of St Stephen.

St Stephen's Hall

The Hall closely matches the dimensions of the old chapel, being 95 ft (28.9 m) long and 30 ft (9.1 m) wide. Brass studs let into the floor indicate the position of the Speaker's Chair and the Table of the House, and two brass tablets in the side walls about 30 ft (9.1 m) from the western end mark the position of the wall which separated the Lobby from the Chamber. It was while passing through this Lobby that Spencer Perceval, the Prime Minister, was shot dead by John Bellingham in 1812.

Statues of famous debaters face one another on either side of the Hall, Clarendon and Hampden, Walpole and Chatham, Pitt and Fox. There are also statues of Falkland (note the broken spur to which a suffragette chained herself in 1908), Somers, Selden, Mansfield, Burke and Grattan. On either side of the doorways are statues of early kings and queens of England.

2   St Stephen's Hall, looking east towards the Central Lobby

Mosaics

At the east and west ends of the Hall are two large mosaic panels by R. Anning Bell, R.A. The one at the east end depicts St Stephen, holding a stone, in allusion to his martyrdom, with King Stephen, traditionally regarded as the founder of the Chapel, clad in mail, on his right, and

Edward the Confessor, the founder of the old Palace of Westminster, kneeling on his left. This mosaic was presented by Sir Joseph Walton, Bt., M.P., and unveiled in 1925. The mosaic at the west end portrays Edward III handing the model of the Chapel he completed to his master mason, Thomas of Canterbury, with representatives of mediaeval craftsmen standing behind the King. It was presented by Sir Robert Houston, Bt., M.P., and was unveiled in 1926.

The ten richly coloured stained glass windows, designed by Pugin and made by Hardman, show the arms of various cities and boroughs. They were restored following damage in Second World War air raids. The Hall was renovated and the war damage repaired in 1960. The five chandeliers were installed in 1978, having been moved from the Committee staircase. They were originally in the Court of Requests.

On 15 August 1945 the Commons met in St Stephen's Hall to enable the new Parliament to be opened in the House of Lords. They also met here on the first day of each session from 1945 to 1950, when they were using the House of Lords for their ordinary sittings. The Hall is now used as an ante-chamber for those waiting to gain admission to the Public Gallery. At the north-west corner is a bookstall selling guidebooks and postcards.

Paintings: The Building of Britain

The walls of the Hall are decorated with panels illustrative of British history, inspired by Speaker Whitley and under the artistic superintendence of Sir David Cameron. They were unveiled on 28 June 1927 by Mr Baldwin, the Prime Minister. They are in chronological order, as follows, clockwise from the north-west corner:

1. King Alfred's long-ships, newly built for the defence of the realm, attack storm-beaten supply vessels of the Danish invaders in Swanage Bay, 877. (Given by the Duke of Devonshire; painted by Colin Gill.)

2. King Richard the First, afterwards called Coeur de Lion, leaves England with an expeditionary force to join the Crusade in Palestine for the recovery of Jerusalem from the Saracens, 11 December 1189. (Given by Viscount Devonport; painted by Glyn Philpot, R.A.)

3. King John, confronted by his barons assembled in force at Runnymede, gives unwilling assent to Magna Carta, 1215. (Given by Viscount Burnham; painted by Charles Sims, R.A.)

4. English people, in spite of many prosecutions for heresy, persist in gathering secretly to read aloud Wycliffe's English version of the Bible. (Given by the Duke of Portland; painted by Sir George Clausen, R.A.)

5. Saint Thomas More, as Speaker of the Commons, in spite of Cardinal Wolsey's imperious demands, refuses to grant King Henry VIII a subsidy without due debate, at Blackfriars, 1523. (Given by Viscount FitzAlan of Derwent; painted by Vivian Forbes.)

6. Queen Elizabeth, the Faerie Queen of her Knights and Merchant Venturers, commissions Sir Walter Raleigh to sail for America and discover new countries, 1584. (Given by the Earl of Derby; painted by A. K. Lawrence, R.A.)

7. Sir Thomas Roe, Envoy from King James the First of England to the Moghul Emperor, succeeds by his courtesy and firmness at the Court of Ajmir in laying the foundation of British influence in India, 1614. (Given by the Duke of Bedford; painted by Sir William Rothenstein.)

8. The English and Scottish Commissioners present to Queen Anne at St James's Palace the articles of agreement for the Parliamentary Union of the two countries, 1707. (Given by Viscount Younger of Leckie; painted by W. T. Monnington, R.A.)

The Chapel of St Mary Undercroft

The Chapel of St Mary Undercroft, sometimes known as the Crypt Chapel, is under St Stephen's Hall (for history, *see* p. 7). It has one of the earliest examples of lierne vaulting, i.e., with non-structural ribs joining the main ribs to form stellar and other patterns.

The Chapel is 90 ft (27.4 m) long, 28 ft (8.5 m) wide and 20 ft (6 m) high and consists of five vaulted bays with moulded ribs, which spring from groups of clustered columns of polished Purbeck marble. The Chapel survived the fire relatively unscathed, and was restored by Edward Barry, son of Sir Charles Barry, between 1860 and 1870, an attempt being made to reproduce the style and tone of the original ornamentation. In particular, the vaulting of stone with its massive ribs and bosses was carefully restored or replaced. During the restoration, the remains of an ecclesiastic were found embalmed in the north wall; they were proved to be those of William Lyndwoode, Bishop of St David's and Keeper of the Privy Seal to Henry VI, who founded a chantry in the Chapel of St

3   The Chapel of St Mary Undercroft, or Crypt Chapel, looking east

4   Boss from the Chapel of St Mary Undercroft: stoning of St Stephen

Stephen, and died in 1464. The Bishop was reburied in the cloister of Westminster Abbey, and his episcopal staff is preserved in the British Museum.

The largest bosses represent the martyrdoms of St Stephen, St John, St Catherine and St Laurence, and St Margaret and the dragon. St Stephen is clad in gorgeous robes and is being stoned by Jews dressed in the costume and long pointed shoes of the fourteenth century. The floor is paved with Minton tiles mixed with marble. The windows are filled with stained glass by John Hardman Powell and are illustrative of the life and death of St Stephen. On the walls the martyrdom of St Stephen is told in the words of the Vulgate. The windows originally in the east end were removed by Barry, and replaced by full length figures on a gold ground, by J. G. Crace & Son, showing St Oswald, St Etheldreda, St Edmund, St Peter, St Stephen, St Edward the Confessor, St Margaret and St Edward the Martyr. On the altar are two nineteenth-century brass candlesticks with bases in the form of kneeling angels, echoed in the kneeling angels at the altar gates and on the pulpit. An Elizabethan silver chalice and paten, made in London in 1571, were presented to the chapel by Members of Parliament in 1946. The beautiful rail and gates at the west end, also designed by Barry, are a splendid example of High Victorian metalwork, and are in the style of the grille made in 1294 for the tomb of Eleanor of Castile in Westminster Abbey.

The octagonal baptistery added by Edward Barry is decorated in harmony with the chapel. At the entrance are incised representations of Noah and his Ark and of Moses holding the Tables of the Law. The pavement is laid with Minton tiles and marbles, having eight incised heads of saints. The bowl of the font is of alabaster, the shafts of Ipplepen marble and the base of Hopton Wood stone and Purbeck marble.

The present main entrance is from Westminster Hall. It was at the bottom of this staircase that a bomb was placed by the Fenians in 1885, and was carried by a policeman into Westminster Hall, where it exploded, blowing out the great window and making a large hole in the floor. At the west end of the chapel is a flight of stairs leading to Old Palace Yard, sometimes used for weddings. It was in the cupboard at the bottom of these stairs that Miss Emily Wilding-Davison, a suffragette, concealed herself for forty-eight hours in order to record her address as the House of Commons in the census of 1911, as a protest against the exclusion of women from the franchise. A plaque commemorates this event.

The chapel has passed through many vicissitudes, having been used at different times as a stable, a coal cellar and as the Speaker's dining room. It is now used for the marriages of Peers and Members and Officers of Parliament, the christenings and marriages of their immediate family, and for celebrations of Holy Communion and other religious services. In 1924 the question of ecclesiastical jurisdiction over the chapel was raised in relation to the rights of a Member of Parliament to have his child baptised by a minister of the Church of Scotland: a subsequent question arose over the possibility of marriage by a Free Church minister. The issue was referred to the Law Officers of the Crown, who decided that no ecclesiastical jurisdiction existed in respect of the Crypt Chapel, and that it was under the sole jurisdiction of the Lord Great Chamberlain (this authority is now also shared with the Lord Chancellor and the Speaker). On 6 July 1978 a Roman Catholic Mass was conducted in the chapel by Cardinal Hume, Archbishop of Westminster, in celebration of the 500th anniversary of the birth of Thomas More.

The Cloisters

The Cloisters to St Stephen's Chapel were rebuilt between 1526 and 1529 in the Perpendicular style at the expense of John Chamber, M.D., Henry VIII's physician, and the last Dean of St Stephen's before its suppression in 1547. The Cloisters consist of two storeys measuring 88 ft by 75 ft (26.8 m by 22.9 m). The lower storey was thoroughly restored after the fire of 1834, the original appearance being faithfully reproduced. The fan vaulting of the roof is of great beauty. Each bay has an elaborately carved central boss, with smaller carved bosses showing Tudor roses, portcullises, fleurs-de-lis and pomegranates. On the west side is a charming oratory. Tradition says the death warrant of Charles I was signed here, but according to the best authorities the majority of the signatures were appended in the Painted Chamber (*see* p. 16). Three sides of this storey are used as writing-rooms for Members. The upper storey of the Cloisters was almost entirely destroyed in the fire of 1834, but was also restored on its ancient lines over a period of years. Considerable damage was caused in the Second World War, after which the south and east sides of the Cloisters were rebuilt with Portland stone faced internally with Caen stone to match the old work. The carving of the vaulting is a fine example of modern craftsmanship.

The wide stone staircase, with a vaulted stone roof in the Perpendicular style, which connects the two storeys on the north side, was designed by Barry as the principal entrance for Members to the House of Commons. On the ground floor of Star Chamber Court, which lies to the north of the Cloisters and takes its name from the old Star Chamber building which stood near by, is the cloak-room through which Members usually enter the building from the Members' Entrance in New Palace Yard. The loop of red tape which hangs from each Member's peg, and which can now be used to hold an umbrella or stick, is a reminder of the days when Members wore swords. The grandfather clock by Vulliamy was already in the Palace before the fire of 1834. A new building on the Westminster Hall side of Star Chamber Court, completed in 1967 at a cost of about £230,000, provides more than 50 offices for Ministers, Members, Officers of the House and the Press.

The Temporary Houses of Parliament, 1835–1851

During the night of 16/17 October 1834 the Palace of Westminster was almost entirely destroyed by a fire, caused by the furnace used to heat the House of Lords being over-stoked with Exchequer tallies. St Stephen's Chapel, the Chamber of the House of Commons, was completely devastated, and the Court of Requests, the Chamber of the House of Lords, was partially destroyed. Some portions of the Palace at the southern end were saved, as well as Westminster Hall and its courtrooms, the Crypt Chapel and parts of Cloister Court at the northern end. On 23 October 1834, the House of Lords assembled in their Library, and the House of Commons in one of the committee rooms belonging to the House of Lords, and Parliament was prorogued.

The House of Commons being a more numerous body than the House of Lords, and the Court of Requests being a wider building than the Painted Chamber, the Painted Chamber was fitted up for the House of Lords, and the Court of Requests for the House of Commons. On 20 June 1835, the sum of £44,000 was voted to defray the expense of providing temporary accommodation for the Houses of Lords and Commons.

The Painted Chamber

The Painted Chamber, which was only partially destroyed by the fire, stood to the south of and parallel with St Stephen's Chapel, facing east and west (*see* plan at end of book). The eastern end corresponded roughly with the present entrance to the Moses Room and looked on to the Cotton Garden and the river. This Chamber was reputed by tradition to have been the bedroom of Edward the Confessor and the room in which he died in 1066, although in fact is likely to have been built with the rest of the larger buildings of the Palace in the twelfth century. Built over an undercroft, it was about 80 ft (24.3 m) long, 28 ft (8.5 m) wide and over 30 ft (9.1 m) high, with three windows in the north wall, two in the south and two in the east. It derived its name from the mass of paintings which decorated its walls. Some of these, including the representation of the Coronation of King Edward the Confessor, were executed under Henry III between 1263 and 1272, and others, from the Old Testament and Book of Maccabees, probably under Edward I from 1292 to 1297; both were under the charge of the painter Walter of Durham. The walls were subsequently covered with whitewash and tapestries.

The discovery that paintings had survived was made in 1799, and between 1818 and 1820 Charles Stothard and Edward Crocker made extensive copies of the paintings discovered, while the Chamber was being repaired for use as the Court of Claims. Reconstructions by Professor Tristram based on these copies can be seen on the stairs leading from the Lower Waiting Hall to the Terrace (*see* p. 61).

Formerly, Parliaments were opened in this Chamber and it was probably here that the death warrant of Charles I was signed. Latterly, the Chamber had been used for conferences between the two Houses and also for special committees. The Lords sat here from 1835 to 1847, when it was demolished. In the reconstruction of 1835 the roof height was raised; the Throne which had been used by George IV at Carlton House was set up at the eastern end; three tiers of seats were arranged on either side of the Chamber; galleries with two tiers of seats, and approached by staircases from the western end of the Chamber, were erected on either side; and the whole was roofed with slates. Above the entrance, facing the Throne, a large gallery was constructed to accommodate strangers and the Press.

The Court of Requests

The Court of Requests, which was formerly known as the White Hall, lay to the south of Westminster Hall on the site where the statue of Richard Coeur de Lion has been erected (*see* plan at end of book). About 80 ft (24.3 m) long, 40 ft (12.1 m) wide and 30 ft (9.1 m) high, it was originally the banqueting hall of the royal palace. It subsequently became the Court of Requests in which petitions of the subjects of the King were heard. The Lords moved into the Court of Requests in 1801 after the Union with Ireland, leaving the ancient building at the southern end of the Palace, which they had occupied for many centuries, and it was demolished in 1823, to make way for Soane's royal approach buildings.

The walls were decorated with a set of ten magnificent Flemish tapestries depicting the defeat of the Spanish Armada in 1588, designed by Hendrik Vroom and woven to the order of Lord Howard of Effingham, Lord High Admiral of England, who sold them to James I in 1612. These were destroyed in the fire of 1834. At the upper end stood the King's Throne, an armed chair profusely carved and gilded, surmounted by a canopy of state. The Commons sat here from 1835 to 1851. The Speaker's Chair was placed at the southern end of the House. There were four tiers of seats at either side and the side galleries had three tiers of seats. At the other end of the Chamber was a gallery for strangers and above the Speaker's Chair was a Press Gallery. The Court of Requests was demolished in 1851.

The New Houses of Parliament

Five months after the fire, in March 1835, a Select Committee of the House of Commons was appointed 'to consider and report upon such plan as may be most fitting and convenient for the permanent accommodation of the Houses of Parliament'. The Committee decided that the style of the new building should be either Gothic or Elizabethan and that the design should be open to general competition, to be judged by specially appointed Commissioners. There were 97 entries, and in March 1836 the winner was announced: Mr (afterwards Sir) Charles Barry, who used the Gothic style of the Tudor period as being in harmony with the old buildings, which were to be preserved and integrated with the new buildings.

The foundation stone of the new Palace was laid (at the angle of the plinth of the Speaker's House nearest the bridge) on 27 April 1840 by Mrs Charles Barry, the wife of the architect. The House of Lords occupied their Chamber on 15 April 1847. The Commons first sat in their Chamber on 30 May 1850 but did not settle in permanently until the opening of the session on 3 February 1852.

The stone used is a magnesian limestone from Anston in Yorkshire. Though suitable for the carving of elaborate gargoyles, statues and the like, it has proved unable to withstand the corroding influences of weather and noxious acids. Renewal of the external masonry has gone on continuously since 1928 except during the Second World War, and work on the perimeter of the building was completed in 1960. A further major programme of repair, restoration and conservation of the stonework was begun in 1981. By 1993 the stonework on the south front, the east or river front, Speaker's Green, New Palace Yard, the west front, the Central Tower and on the Clock Tower had been freed of the effects of corrosion and grime. The cleaning of the Victoria Tower is due to be completed in 1994, at a cost of around £7.5 million: the scaffolding on the tower weighs almost 690 tons (701 tonnes) and requires support some 68 ft (20.7 m) below ground level. Thereafter, the stonework in the internal courtyards is to be repaired, restored and cleaned.

The Palace is built on a bed of concrete up to 10 ft (3 m) thick, covers an area of 8 acres (3.2 ha), has over 1,100 rooms, 100 staircases, 35 passenger lifts and 2 miles (3.2 km) of passages, and cost over £2 million pounds to build. Electric lighting was installed in the Lords Chamber in 1883, in the dials of the clock in 1906, and in the Commons Chamber in 1912. The total superficial area of masonry is about 900,000 sq ft (83,610 sq m) and there are about 775,000 cu ft (21,948 cu m) of stone. There are over 300 statues on the main façades of the building, representing saints and the kings and queens of England from the Norman Conquest to the reign of Queen Victoria, many of them life size. The statues on the arcade of the west front of New Palace Yard are of Portland stone and were executed in 1866 by H. Armstead, R.A. The remainder were carved in Anston stone by J. Thomas and his assistants; many of these statues have been renewed in Clipsham stone. The general roof-level is about 70 ft (21.3 m) from the ground, with many ornate turrets dominated by the Victoria Tower at the south end, the Clock Tower at the north end, and the Central Tower in the centre of the building.

The north front of the Palace, from the Clock Tower to the river, is 232 ft (70.7 m) in length and overlooks Speaker's Green, which terminates in the Speaker's Steps leading to the river. This portion of the building is occupied by the official residences of the Speaker and the Serjeant at Arms. The Speaker's House contains a suite of State Rooms, with much of the original Victorian furniture, including the original State Bed

5   The Speaker's State Bed

recovered by the National Heritage Memorial Fund from private ownership in 1981, and also the magnificent collection of portraits of Speakers begun by Speaker Addington in 1803.

The south front from the Victoria Tower to the river is 322 ft (98.1 m) in length and overlooks the Victoria Tower Gardens. It contains the Queen's Robing Room, the Lord Chancellor's offices and his official residence, and has statues of kings and queens of England in the divisions between the windows.

The east or river front is 872 ft (265.7 m) long, including the Terrace, which is 678 ft (206.6 m) long and 33 ft (10 m) wide. The front is decorated with the arms of the kings and queens of England, from William the Conqueror to Queen Victoria, at the level of the principal floor, and many statues, the uppermost being one of Queen Victoria. From the Terrace a good view is obtained of Lambeth Palace, St Thomas's Hospital, County Hall (the headquarters of the former Greater London Council) and the tower of the Shell building. In 1971–72 the level of the Terrace and its parapet was raised as a precaution against flooding. On 16 July 1986, 100 rowing eights took part in a regatta along the river front to raise funds for the restoration of St Margaret's Church.

The west front, extending from the Clock Tower to the Victoria Tower, is roughly divided into two halves by a line running through the Central Tower and St Stephen's Entrance. The northern half of the building is occupied by the House of Commons, the southern half by the House of Lords. The northern half incorporates the buildings saved from the fire of 1834, and contains the Clock Tower, New Palace Yard (the entrance for Members of the House of Commons) and Westminster Hall.

Beneath New Palace Yard is a five-level underground car park, with space for 450 cars, which was constructed in 1972–74 at a cost of £2.5 million. An archaeological investigation undertaken in 1971–72 revealed the octagonal base of a large canopied fountain built in 1443 to celebrate Henry VI's attainment of his majority; incorporating the remains of an earlier twelfth-century conduit, it stood in the Yard until the late seventeenth century. It was on the exit ramp of this car park that Airey Neave, M.P., was assassinated on 30 March 1979 by a bomb planted in his car by Irish terrorists. The modern landscaping of the Yard incorporates a formal avenue of limes, benches of Portland stone and an octagonal pool and fountain with Portland stone surround marking the site of the Tudor fountain. In this pool stands a welded steel sculpture by Walenty Pytel, depicting the beasts and birds of six continents, topped by St Stephen's Crown, commissioned in 1977 in commemoration of H.M. The Queen's Silver Jubilee as a gift from Members of the House of Commons. On the north of the Yard are six aged catalpa trees and three younger ones on the west side. The canopy of the Members' entrance is made of cast aluminium and was completed in 1976. The Yard has gas lamps, automatically lit and extinguished.

The western side of Westminster Hall received its present form in 1888 (after the removal of the Law Courts to the Strand in 1882), when the sunken garden was made, Richard II's flying buttresses were exposed to view, and the Grand Committee Room annexe, designed by John Pearson, was built. A statue of Oliver Cromwell by Hamo Thornycroft, presented by Lord Rosebery in 1899, occupies the centre of the sunk garden.

The southern half of the west front, from St Stephen's Entrance to the Victoria Tower, perhaps the most elegant façade of the whole building, contains the Peers' Entrance, in the centre, surmounted by a small tower. This front and the south side of St Stephen's Entrance form two sides of Old Palace Yard, the south-west corner of which is indicated by the Jewel Tower, built by Henry Yevele in 1365–66 to house the King's private treasure. Subsequently used to store parliamentary records and, from 1869 to 1938, for testing weights and measures, it was restored in 1948–56 and now contains a permanent exhibition on Parliament Past and Present. In the Yard stands a fine equestrian statue of Richard Coeur de Lion by Marochetti, erected in 1860.

The Palace contains eleven open courtyards with a narrow carriage-way joining Speaker's Court at the north end to Royal Court at the south end.

The whole Palace is lavishly decorated both externally and internally with the monogram VR and countless emblems of historic connections of the Royal Family. Most of the elaborate detail of the fittings and furniture is due to the graceful fancy of Augustus Welby Pugin. The differentiation between red furnishings in the Lords and green in the Commons has historical roots. Red, the traditional colour of royalty, has been the colour of the House of Lords since at least the beginning of the sixteenth century: the use of green in the Commons dates from a century later.

In 1841 a Royal Commission on the Fine Arts was set up under the presidency of the Prince Consort 'to consider whether by the building of the New Palace of Westminster the opportunity should not be taken to encourage the art of painting and sculpture in its decoration'. Certain schemes were agreed upon and prizes were offered for the best cartoons to illustrate the history of the British Isles; £4,000 a year was spent on these objects for 20 years, but on the death of the Prince Consort in 1861 the Commission ceased to enter into new agreements. Little further was done for about 45 years until Lewis Harcourt, as First Commissioner of Works, encouraged the presentation of pictures and prints by Members of the House, with the result that the Palace now possesses a fine collection of prints of the old Palace and of prime ministers and famous statesmen. Speaker Whitley continued the good work and saw to the completion of the mosaics in the Central Lobby and of the mosaics and mural paintings in St Stephen's Hall. In recent years, renewed efforts have been made by both Houses to decorate, refurbish and conserve the Palace and its treasures.

The Clock Tower

The Clock Tower rises 316 ft (96.3 m) from Thames level as marked by Trinity House to the top of the finial and is about 40 ft (12.1 m) square; the top of the spire is 9 in (22.8 cm) out of the vertical; 334 stairs lead up to the belfry; there is no lift. In the lower part of the Tower are the rooms in which persons were confined when 'committed to the custody of the Serjeant at Arms'. Charles Bradlaugh was the last Member so committed in the year 1880. The tower is often referred to as 'Big Ben', more properly the nickname of the hour bell. This bell is generally supposed to have been named after Sir Benjamin Hall, who was First Commissioner of Works when it was hung. More probably it was named after Benjamin Caunt, the prize fighter, who fought his last fight in 1857. He was then 42 years old, weighed 17 stone (107.9 kg), and fought 60 rounds to draw.

The present Clock Tower stands near the site of the clock tower which was built by Henry Yevele, the architect of Westminster Hall, in 1365 and was pulled down soon after 1698 under the direction of Sir Christopher Wren. The bell, known over the centuries as 'Great Tom of Westminster', now hangs in the north-west tower of St Paul's Cathedral. Now known as 'Great Tom of St Paul's', it has deputised for Big Ben on the BBC's radio services on occasions when the chiming gear at Westminster has been under repair. Since 1885 a light at the top of the tower, called the Ayrton

Light after the First Commissioner of Works of that name, has indicated when either House is sitting at night; it was extinguished for most of the Second World War. The tower was first floodlit in September 1931 for the International Illumination Congress, and subsequently for occasional celebrations. Since 1964 it has been floodlit all the year round.

The Clock

The installation of the clock and bells was not accomplished without a great deal of controversy. Eventually, in 1852, a contract was given to E. J. Dent, maker of astronomical clocks, to make the clock designed by Professor George Airy, Astronomer Royal, and Edmund Beckett Denison, Q.C. (afterwards Lord Grimthorpe). Dent died in the following year, but the contract was completed by his stepson and successor, Frederick Dent, and the clock was fixed in the tower and began its service on 31 May 1859. An inscription carved on the north face of the tower commemorates the centenary of this event. E. Dent and Co. retained the responsibility for the winding and minor maintenance of the clock mechanism until 1971, when it was assumed by the clockmakers Thwaites and Reed.

The dials of the clock are 23 ft (7 m) in diameter, each face containing 312 panes of opalescent glass, cleaned every three years. The figures are 2 ft (60 cm) long and the minute spaces 1 ft (30.4 cm) square; the figures were designed by Pugin, with 4 shown as IV rather than the horologist's traditional IIII. The minute hands of hollow copper are 14 ft (4.2 m) long and weigh 2 cwt (101.6 kg); the hour hands of gun-metal are 9 ft (2.7 m) long and weigh about 6 cwt (304.8 kg); the pendulum is 14 ft (4.2 m) long; beating 2 seconds, and the bob of the pendulum weighs about 4 cwt (203.2 kg); the weights of the clock weigh nearly 2½ tons. The weights are raised from nearly ground level by an electric motor.

The mechanism of the clock weighs 5 tons. The escapement is known as the 'Grimthorpe double three-legged gravity', which has become almost standard practice in good public clocks. The great feature of this escapement is that external influences such as wind pressures on the hands are not communicated to the pendulum, and therefore a constant rate of timekeeping is assured.

The clock is not automatically synchronized or controlled in any way. Corrections, necessary to allow for changes in barometric pressure, etc., are made by adjusting the weights in the tray at the top of the pendulum. The addition of one old penny causes the clock to gain two fifths of a second in 24 hours. From 1863 to 1940 it telegraphed its performance by special line twice daily to the Astronomer Royal at Greenwich. His last annual report showed that on only 16 days in the previous nine months had the clock been more than one second off time.

Stoppages of the clock have been rare, apart from overhaul and changing to and from Summer Time. The worst breakdown in the history of the clock occurred at 3.45 a.m. on 5 August 1976. Metal fatigue in the governor of the chiming gear released the control of the 1-ton weights, which increased the speed of the barrel from its normal 1½ r.p.m. to some 1,600 r.p.m. The barrel, weighing ½ ton, was thrown out by centrifugal force, smashed through the mechanism, fracturing the main frame, and flew through the air until it hit the wall of the Clock Room. The clock was restarted shortly after 4 p.m. the same day, but the striking of the hour bell was not resumed until 27 August. Subsequent investigation by staff of the Atomic Energy Research Establishment at Harwell revealed a number of other weaknesses, and as a result nearly half the clock mechanism was replaced. The clock resumed chiming at noon on 4 May 1977 on the occasion of the visit of H.M. The Queen for her Silver Jubilee Address. The hour chime was suspended in mid-1990 to permit the construction of a new hammer arm, and in mid-1992 the quarter hour chimes were silent as a result of the replacement of the chime main wheel.

Bells

The four quarter bells (of which the smallest – G Sharp – weighs just over a ton and the largest – B Natural – nearly 4 tons) were cast by Messrs. Warner at their London foundry in Cripplegate. The hour-bell – E Natural – weighing more than 16½ tons; was cast in their foundry at Stockton-on-Tees, and was brought to London by sea from West Hartlepool in October 1856. It was then hung on a gallows where it was rung for a quarter of an hour each week for ten months.

A year later (October 1857) a crack 4 ft (1.2 m) long extending from the sound bow to the waist was discovered. The contract for recasting was given to George Mears of Whitechapel, who successfully carried out the work in April 1858. The bell, now weighing 13½ tons, was hung in the

6   John Darwin, who was responsible for the reconstruction of the clock
    after it broke down in 1976, stands inside the clockface of Big Ben

Clock Tower in October 1858 and began to be used in July 1859. After a few months an 11 in (28 cm) crack appeared, and for three years the hour was struck on the fourth quarter bell. In 1862 Professor Airy recommended that the bell should be given a quarter of a turn so that a different part should be struck, and that the weight of the hammer should be reduced. This was done, and the original hammer is to be seen in the lobby at the foot of the Terrace Stairs (*see* p. 61). In 1957 all the bells were re-hung and the hammer work was renewed at the Whitechapel Foundry.

The chimes are the same as those which were erected in the Church of St Mary the Great at Cambridge in 1793–94 and, in a slightly different sequence, at the Royal Exchange in 1845. They are traditionally associated with the lines: 'Lord, through this hour, Be thou our guide, That by Thy power, No foot shall slide.' The tune by Dr Jowett and Dr Crotch is said to be based on a phrase in the accompaniment of Handel's 'I know that my Redeemer liveth' and is as follows:

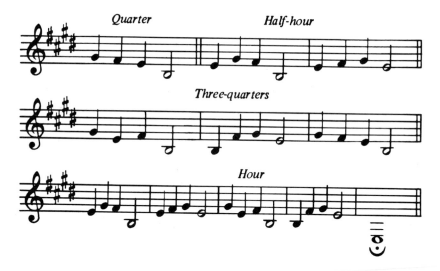

Big Ben was tolled for the first time for the funeral of King Edward VII in 1910 and again for the funerals of King George V and King George VI in 1936 and 1952. The bells were silent from 9.45 a.m. until midnight on 30 January 1965, the day of Sir Winston Churchill's funeral. The BBC broadcast the New Year chimes for the first time on 1 January 1924. The live broadcasting of the chimes through the years of the Second World War on both the Home and Overseas Programmes made them known worldwide as a symbol of British democracy. From June to September

1944, however, recordings were played, to ensure that the sound of explosions at a very accurately measured time would not assist the enemy in setting the targets for flying bombs.

The Houses of Parliament in the Second World War

During the Second World War the Houses of Parliament were damaged by air raids on fourteen different occasions.

On 26 September 1940 a high-explosive bomb which fell in Old Palace Yard caused severe damage to the south wall of St Stephen's Porch, the tracery of the great window in this wall, the War Memorial under the window and the masonry of the West Front. The statue of Richard Coeur de Lion appeared to have been lifted bodily from the pedestal but sustained only minor damage, the sword being bent.

On 8 December 1940 a high-explosive bomb demolished the south and east sides of the Cloisters and did considerable damage to the other two sides.

The raid on 10 May 1941, it is now known from the records of the Luftwaffe, was not a deliberate attack on the Houses of Parliament. At least twelve incidents are recorded on this night in various parts of the building, and three people were killed. The Commons Chamber was entirely destroyed by a fire which spread to the Members' Lobby and caused the ceiling to collapse. The roof of Westminster Hall was also set on fire. Part of the lantern and a considerable area of the roof boarding and rafters were destroyed, but the trusses do not appear to have suffered to any great extent. A small bomb or an anti-aircraft shell struck the Clock Tower at the eaves of the metal roof and destroyed some of the ornamental ironwork and damaged the stonework. All the glass in the south clock face was broken, but the clock and bells were undamaged and the chimes were broadcast as usual. The House of Lords was struck by a bomb which passed through the floor of the Chamber without exploding. The north side of Peers' Court, the Government and Opposition Whips' Offices, and a number of other rooms were destroyed.

Alternative accommodation was provided for both Houses in Church House, and they sat there for short periods during the winter of 1940–41 (including the State Opening of Parliament on 21 November 1940), from April to June 1941 and from June to August 1944 during the flying-bomb attacks. The Lords sat in the Hall of Convocation; the Commons sat in the Hoare Memorial Hall, where a tablet commemorates their occupation. For most of the period from 1941 to 1951 the Commons sat in the House of Lords and the Lords in the Robing Room (*see* pp. 32–3).

The Rebuilding of the House of Commons

In December 1943 a Select Committee was appointed 'to consider and report upon plans for the rebuilding of the House of Commons and upon such alterations as may be considered desirable while preserving all its essential features'. The Committee, chaired by Earl Winterton, M.P., selected Sir Giles Gilbert Scott, O.M., R.A., as the architect and Dr Oscar Faber as the engineer. The scheme prepared by these gentlemen was approved by the Royal Fine Art Commission, recommended by the Committee, and agreed to by the House on 25 January 1945.

Clearance began on 10 May 1945 and by August of the following year the steel frame was complete. The main contract was let by the Ministry of Works to John Mowlem & Co. The foundation stone was laid by Mr Speaker on 26 May 1948. The total cost of the new building was £2 million. The Commons met in their new Chamber for the first time on 26 October 1950. Among those present in the Gallery were the Speakers or Presiding Officers of the Legislatures of twenty-eight countries of the Commonwealth.

In addition to more seats within the Chamber, the new building utilizes the space above and below the Chamber to provide accommodation which was not available in the old building. Below the Chamber on the ground floor there are sixteen Ministers' rooms and two Ministers' conference rooms. On the lower ground floor there are secretarial, conference, and interview rooms for the use of Members. Above the Chamber are the Public Bill Office and the Journal Office, and other offices of the Department of the Clerk of the House.

Since 1963 much additional accommodation has been provided for Lords, Members and staff, notably above the Members' tea room and Lords' dining room, in the roof space above the committee rooms on the east front and in the new buildings in State Officers' Court and Star

Chamber Court (*see* p. 15), as well as in the upper reaches of the Speaker's House and in vacated official residences. Further accommodation has been made available outside the Palace, notably in the Norman Shaw North and South buildings (known, when the headquarters of the Metropolitan Police, as New Scotland Yard), in Dean's Yard near Westminster Abbey and in offices on Millbank.

After many years of discussions and proposals, the House of Commons agreed, on 22 November 1983, to the first phase of a complex proposal to redevelop the site between Parliament Street, Bridge Street and the Victoria Embankment.

This phase, covering the area bounded by Parliament Street, Derby Gate, Canon Row and Bridge Street, was completed in March 1991 at a cost of around £40 million. The southern section, formerly Nos. 34–42 Parliament Street and St Stephen's Tavern, and now known collectively as 1 Parliament Street, provides offices for Members and their staff and other facilities, including a cafeteria named Bellamy's in commemoration of the former caterers to the House of Commons. A parliamentary bookshop has also been opened on the corner of Bridge Street and Parliament Street. No. 1 Parliament Street is decorated with specially commissioned paintings of recent political figures by Henry Mee and Graham Jones, the ten-year rule (*see* p. 62) having been suspended for buildings outside the Palace, and with watercolour scenes of stately homes, seaside resorts, etc.; at the entrance is a vast bronze portcullis. The two buildings in the centre of the site, formerly 43 and 44 Parliament Street, now numbered 2 and 3, have been converted into official residences and sleeping accommodation. The northern half, known as 1 Derby Gate, contains the converted premises of the Whitehall Club, built in 1866, and houses a branch library for Members and their staff and the Research Division of the House of Commons Library.

Plans for the development of Phase 2, the area between Phase 1 and the Victoria Embankment, were approved in 1991, based on a six-storey rectangular building, to be constructed on a concrete raft over Westminster Underground Station, around an open courtyard. The design, by Michael Hopkins and Partners, is intended to provide offices for around 230 Members and their staff, as well as offices for Select Committee staff and three additional Select Committee rooms, at a cost of around £60 million. A final Phase 3 is to cover the former police station at Canon Row and the refurbishment of Norman Shaw South.

The House of Lords

Victoria Tower

The Victoria Tower is 323 ft (98.4 m) high to the base of the flagstaff, 73 ft (22.2 m) high in addition, and 75 ft (22.8 m) square. The main structure of the Tower was completed in 1858. It was for many years the tallest square building in the world; since 1966 it has been floodlit at night. Here are stored the records of Parliament, numbering some three million documents, among them the master copies of all Acts of Parliament since 1497 (*see* p. 44). The Union Jack is flown from the Tower from 10 a.m. to sunset on sitting days, and on certain special occasions such as royal birthdays. Three sizes of flag are in use, the largest being 36 ft (10.9 m) by 18 ft (5.4 m). On 20 April 1917 the 'Stars and Stripes' was flown alongside the Union Jack to celebrate the entry of the U.S.A. into the First World War. When the Sovereign comes to open Parliament the Royal Standard is broken from the flagstaff, and it is replaced by the Union Jack after the ceremony. The Royal Carriage drives under the great archway, 50 ft (15.2 m) high, to the entrance leading to the Royal Staircase. The interior of this archway is decorated with the statues of the patron saints of England, Scotland and Ireland, a life-size statue of Queen Victoria and two allegorical figures of Justice and Mercy.

Royal Staircase and Norman Porch

The Royal Staircase, nearly 15 ft (4.5 m) wide, consists of a broad flight of 26 grey granite steps of 5½ in (13.9 cm) rise under a stone vault. The royal coats of arms on either side of the staircase, believed to have come from the old Palace, were placed here in 1954. The lobby at its top is known as the Norman Porch because of the original intention to place statues of the

Norman kings there. Instead, there is a collection of portrait busts of 16 prime ministers who have sat in the House of Lords, the most recent one being that of Lord Home of the Hirsel by Michael Black, unveiled on 8 March 1983. The portraits are of Queen Victoria by W. A. Menzies, after Benjamin Constant, and of the Duke of Wellington by John Lucas. The two panels of fine Victorian glass show Edward the Confessor and the young Queen Victoria.

The Queen's Robing Room

The Queen's Robing Room, designed entirely for the ceremonial route taken by the Queen at the State Opening of Parliament, is 54 ft (16.4 m) long, 37 ft (11.2 m) wide and 25 ft (7.6 m) high, with two carved doorways ornamented with fine metal work. An oak dado runs round the room with 18 panels of deep carving, by H. Armstead, portraying stories from the legend of King Arthur, as told in Malory's *Morte d'Arthur*. Above the dado are five large pictures, also from the legend of King Arthur, by William Dyce, R.A. They illustrate in true fresco the virtues of Chivalry: *Generosity* (King Arthur, unhorsed by Sir Tristram, is spared by the intervention of Sir Lancelot), *Religion* (Vision of Sir Galahad, Sir Percival and his sister and Sir Boris), and *Courtesy* (Sir Tristram harping to La Belle Isolde), all of which were finished between 1851 and 1852, and *Mercy* (Sir Gawaine, having slain a lady, swears not to do so again) in 1854. *Hospitality* (Admission of Sir Tristram to the fellowship of the Round Table) remained unfinished on Dyce's death in 1864, and was completed by C. W. Cope, R.A. in 1865. Two other large frescoes illustrating *Fidelity* and *Courage* were originally intended but never undertaken; portraits of Queen Victoria and the Prince Consort by Winterhalter hang in the place intended for them.

The border of the inlaid floor is decorated with heraldic devices showing the portcullis, the rose and the lion; on the shields in the frieze are blazoned the arms of the Knights of the Round Table. The fireplace is made of marbles of various colours from the British Isles, with a metal statuette on either side, one of St George fighting the Dragon, the other of St Michael. On a dais at the end of the room is a Chair of State beneath a canopy carved with the rose of England, the thistle of Scotland, the shamrock of Ireland, and Queen Victoria's monogram. No furniture was envisaged for the room: the gilded chairs designed by Pugin are recent

7 The Robing Room: *Religion*, or *The Vision of Sir Galahad*, by William Dyce

loans. The cloth at the back of the dais was embroidered with the Royal Arms and the Queen's monogram by the Royal School of Needlework in 1856. The Victorian glass is by J. Hardman Powell.

In 1931, the Joint Committee of Lords and Commons on East Africa sat in the Robing Room and the Burma Round Table Conference was opened here by the Prince of Wales; and in 1933, the Joint Committee on Indian Constitutional Reform met in the Room.

In 1941, when the Commons Chamber was destroyed, the Lords gave up their own Chamber to the Commons and sat in the Robing Room, which was fitted up for their use. From 1941 to 1944 the Sessions of Parliament were opened here. Two State Chairs were placed on the existing dais and a smaller replica of the Woolsack was placed in the appropriate position. Three tiers of benches upholstered in red were installed, with two gangways. At each side of the room panelled screens were erected to form Division Lobbies. At the west end (over the fireplace) a gallery was built for reporters and strangers, and the space below this gallery was formed into the Bar of the House with seats for peeresses and distinguished strangers. The Lords returned to their own Chamber on 29 May 1951.

8   The Robing Room, looking east towards the Throne

The Royal Gallery

The Royal Gallery, through which the Sovereign progresses for the State Opening of Parliament, is impressive for its proportions: 110 ft (33.5 m) long, 45 ft (13.7 m) wide and 45 ft (13.7 m) high. Beyond its role as a processional gallery, however, it has little functional purpose.

9 The Royal Gallery

The side walls are decorated by two large pictures, 45 ft (13.7 m) by
12 ft (3.6 m), painted by Daniel Maclise, R.A., representing the meeting
of Wellington and Blücher after the Battle of Waterloo in 1815, and the
death of Nelson at Trafalgar in 1805, with life-size figures. The pictures
were painted in the water-glass process. The former was finished in 1861
and the latter in 1865, the painting of the two pictures having taken over
seven years. The authenticity of the depiction of the meeting of
Wellington and Blücher at the ruined inn, La Belle Alliance, including the
informal forage cap worn by Blücher, was attested by General Nostitz,
former aide-de-camp to Blücher, following an inquiry by Queen Victoria.

Maclise was to have painted scenes of nineteen further historical
paintings to fill the rest of the Gallery, and sketches for paintings of Queen
Elizabeth at Tilbury and Admiral Blake at Tunis survive. In 1864 however
the Fine Arts Commissioners decided to wind up current commissions.

The colours have faded over the years, and have been restored on a number of occasions. In 1925 the first Earl of lveagh offered to complete the decoration of the Royal Gallery, as part of the scheme for a House of Lords war memorial; but the Royal Fine Art Commission reported in 1930 that the panels designed by Sir Frank Brangwyn, R.A. which represented the British Empire, mainly through its flora and fauna, would not harmonise with their surroundings. The House of Lords upheld this view on 3 April 1930 by a vote of 55 to 11. The panels now adorn the Assembly Hall of the Swansea Corporation.

The royal portraits around the walls are of George I, George II and Queen Caroline, after Sir Godfrey Kneller; George III and Queen Charlotte after Reynolds; George IV after Sir Thomas Lawrence; William IV and Queen Adelaide, attributed to Sir William Beechey; Edward VII after Sir Luke Fildes, and Queen Alexandra and George V by the same artist; Queen Mary after Sir William Llewellyn; George VI and Queen Elizabeth the Queen Mother after Sir Gerald Kelly; Queen Elizabeth II by Sir James Gunn; and Prince Philip, Duke of Edinburgh, by A. C. Davidson-Houston. Beside the doorways and the bay window are four pairs of gilded stone statues by John Philip: King Alfred and William I; Richard I and Edward III; Henry V and Queen Elizabeth I; and William III and Queen Anne. The original stained-glass windows were blown out by bomb blast; the present ones are recreations from Pugin's original cartoons.

On the panelling in the south-east corner are recorded the names of members of the House of Lords and their sons who gave their lives in the two world wars; and three volumes in a glass case in the bay window commemorate the 408 Peers, Lords of Parliament and Officers of the House of Lords who laid down their lives during the First and Second World Wars. In front of this case is a block of timber from the jetty used during the evacuation of Dunkirk by the British Expeditionary Force in 1940. In the south-east corner is a model of the Palace of Westminster as it was in the reign of Henry VIII. In the south-west corner is a display cabinet showing a small selection of the historic documents held by the House of Lords Record Office, including the death warrant of Charles I and the draft Declaration of Rights of 1689.

The Royal Gallery was used for the trial of Earl Russell by his peers in 1901 and the trial of Lord de Clifford by his peers in 1935. The former was convicted of bigamy; the latter acquitted of manslaughter, a charge arising out of a motor accident. Following the fall of a boss from the ceiling of the House of Lords on 21 July 1980 (*see* p. 41), the House sat in the Royal Gallery from 22 July until the adjournment for the summer recess on 8 August. It has also been used for a number of parliamentary ceremonies and, in particular, for the reception of visiting statesmen. Addresses from both Houses of Parliament were presented to King George V on 19 November 1918 on the signing of the armistice, and to King George VI on 17 May and 21 August 1945 on the conclusion of the Second World War in Europe and Japan respectively.

The President of the French Republic and Mme Auriol were welcomed here by both Houses of Parliament on 9 March 1950; and receptions were given for H.I.M. Haile Selassie, Emperor of Ethiopia, on 22 October 1954, and for Mr Bulganin and Mr Khrushchev on 24 April 1956. Both Houses of Parliament were addressed by Field Marshal Smuts on 21 October 1942; Mr Mackenzie King, Prime Minister of Canada, on 11 May 1944; U Thant, Secretary-General of the United Nations, on 28 April 1966; Mr Kosygin, Prime Minister of the USSR, on 9 February 1967; Signor Saragat, President of Italy, on 28 April 1969; Herr Willy Brandt, Chancellor of West Germany, on 3 March 1970; M. Giscard d'Estaing, President of France, on 23 June 1976; Ronald Reagan, President of the United States of America, on 8 June 1982; M. François Mitterand, President of France, on 24 October 1984; King Juan Carlos of Spain on 23 April 1986; Herr Richard von Weiszäcker, President of West Germany, on 2 July 1986; Signor Cossiga, President of Italy, on 24 October 1990; and Mr Boris Yeltsin, President of the Russian Federation, on 10 November 1992.

The Prince's Chamber

The Prince's Chamber serves as an ante-room to the House of Lords, and is called after the apartment of that name which adjoined the ancient House of Lords. (*See* plan at end of book.) Twelve bas-reliefs, executed in bronze by William Theed between 1855 and 1857, commemorate historic events of the Tudor period:

1. The visit of the Emperor Charles V to Henry VIII.

2. Edward VI granting a charter to Christ's Hospital.

3. Lady Jane Grey at her studies.

4. Sebastian Cabot visiting Henry VII.

5. Catherine of Aragon pleading her cause.

6. The Field of the Cloth of Gold.

7. Sir Walter Raleigh spreading his cloak for Queen Elizabeth.

8. Queen Elizabeth knighting Francis Drake.

9. The death of Sir Philip Sidney.

10. Mary Queen of Scots leaving France.

11. The escape of Mary Queen of Scots from Loch Leven Castle.

12. The murder of Rizzio.

10 The Prince's Chamber, showing Gibson's statue of Queen Victoria

The painted Tudor portraits, set in panels around the Chamber, were executed under the supervision of Richard Burchett by the students of the Royal School of Art, South Kensington, and depict: Henry VII of Lancaster and Elizabeth of York; Prince Arthur and Catherine of Aragon; Henry VIII, Anne Boleyn, Jane Seymour, Anne of Cleves, Catherine Howard and Katherine Parr; Edward VI; Queen Mary and Philip of Spain; Queen Elizabeth; Louis XII of France and Princess Mary; Charles Brandon, Duke of Suffolk; The Marchioness of Dorset; Lady Jane Grey and Lord Guilford Dudley; James IV of Scotland and Princess Margaret; the Earl of Angus; James V and Mary of Guise; Mary Queen of Scots, Francis II of France and Lord Darnley. Above these panel portraits is a frieze carved with the armorial bearings, gilded and coloured, of the kings and queens of England, with their names carved alongside.

The six panels at window level were intended to contain copies of the Armada tapestries, lost in the fire of 1834.

The six stained-glass windows by Carl Edwards, which replace those destroyed in the Second World War, were given by the late Lord Kenilworth and contain among others of the same period the arms of Henry VII and Elizabeth of York, Henry VIII and Catherine of Aragon, Philip of Spain and Mary, Lord Darnley and Mary, Queen of Scots.

The dominating feature of the Chamber is the massive marble statue by John Gibson, R.A., of Queen Victoria with flanking figures of Justice and Clemency, erected in 1856. The panels of the pedestal represent Commerce, Science and Industry. Queen Victoria holds a sceptre and a laurel crown. The image of Truth hangs around Justice's neck; Clemency proffers an olive branch, her sword sheathed. The throne is ornamented with lions and sea horses. The two octagonal tables and other furniture were constructed by J. Webb to Pugin's designs.

The Chamber
of the House of Lords

The Chamber of the House of Lords is 80 ft (24.3 m) long, 45 ft (13.7 m) wide, and 45 ft (13.7 m) high.

The Throne canopy, designed by Pugin, is divided into three compartments. At the opening of Parliament, when the brass rail is

11 The Chamber of the House of Lords, looking south towards the
Throne canopy

removed, the Queen and Prince Philip sit on Chairs of State in the centre compartment, which is decorated with the royal arms, surmounted by panels with the badges of the parts of the United Kingdom. Above are plaster statuettes of St George and four knights, holding the badges of the four principal orders of chivalry: St Patrick, the Garter, the Thistle and the Bath. The Prince of Wales sits in the compartment on the Queen's right, decorated with the arms of Edward VII when Prince of Wales, and surmounted by panels with the badge of three ostrich feathers and the motto *Ich Dien*. Princess Anne, the Princess Royal, if present, sits in the compartment on the Queen's left, decorated with the arms of Prince Albert, the Prince Consort, and surmounted by panels with his German heraldic badges of Marck, Thuringia, Meissen, Saxony, Julich and Berg. In the outer spandrels of the canopy over the central compartment are carvings of St George and the Dragon. The Throne canopy was thoroughly cleaned, restored and regilded in 1985 and 1986.

In front of the Throne is the Woolsack, where the Lord Chancellor sits as Speaker of the House of Lords, with the Mace behind him. The Woolsack is traditionally held to have been placed in the House in the reign of Edward III. Records of the House of Lords show 'that the judges shall sit upon woolsacks', and in Elizabethan times standing orders refer to 'sacks, whereon the judges sit'. In course of time the Woolsack came to be stuffed with hair, but in 1938 it was restuffed with a blend of English, Welsh, Scottish and Northern Irish wool, and wool from the Commonwealth countries, given by the International Wool Secretariat. In front of the Chancellor's Woolsack are two woolsacks where the Judges sit at the opening of Parliament, and in front of them again is the Table of the House, built by J. Webb to Pugin's design, with chairs for three Clerks, and a table for the official reporters. For a description of the House of Lords in session, see p. 71.

At the north end of the Chamber is the Bar of the House. The Commons with their Speaker stand below the Bar on ceremonial occasions, such as the opening and prorogation of a Session, a reminder that Parliament was originally a single assembly of which they were part.

Frescoes

At either end of the Chamber are three arches filled with frescoes completed between 1846 and 1849. Those above the Throne represent:

1. Edward III conferring the Order of the Garter on the Black Prince, by C. W. Cope.

2. The baptism of King Ethelbert, by W. Dyce.

3. Prince Henry acknowledging the authority of Judge Gascoigne, by C. W. Cope.

Those above the Strangers' Gallery, reflecting in abstract form the subject matter of the historical subjects, depict:

1. The Spirit of Justice, by Daniel Maclise.

2. The Spirit of Religion, by J. C. Horsley.

3. The Spirit of Chivalry, by Daniel Maclise.

Decoration

The six windows on either side of the Chamber, before they were blown out by bomb blast, contained stained glass portraits of kings and queens of England and Scotland, designed by Pugin and made by Ballantyne & Allen of Edinburgh. A trial window showing William the Conqueror survives (*see* p. 45). The new stained glass, designed in the 1950s by Carl Edwards, shows the coats of arms of peers of the period 1360–1900 and was given by Lord Kenilworth. Between the windows and at the end of the Chamber are bronze statues of the sixteen barons and two archbishops who forced King John to assent to Magna Carta; under the side galleries are carved oak pillars surmounted by small carved busts of the kings of England. Beneath the side galleries are painted the armorial bearings of the Sovereigns from Edward III and of the Lord Chancellors of England from 1377; below the Strangers' Gallery are the arms of the various archbishoprics and bishoprics, and the arms of the Saxon, Norman, Plantagenet, Tudor, Stuart and Hanoverian Royal Houses.

Ceiling

The ceiling of the House is divided into eighteen compartments, showing many ancient royal and national emblems. On 21 July 1980 an ornamented wooden boss fell onto an empty bench during a sitting of the House. Examination showed that nothing more than glue had been used during construction of the Chamber to attach these ornaments and, more seriously, that heat and pollution from the nineteenth-century gas light

41

fittings had caused serious deterioration of the roof timbers. An artificial ceiling was built to enable extensive repairs to be made without having to close the Chamber. The repairs were completed by October 1984, at a cost of £1.5 million.

At the front of the Press Gallery, above the clock, is the commentary box constructed in 1976 for the purpose of sound broadcasting of the House's proceedings. Televising the proceedings of the House was first permitted on a six-month experimental basis with effect from 23 January 1985. Since 12 May 1986 proceedings have been televised on a regular basis and, since 1992, by five remote-control cameras.

Temporary House of Commons

From May 1941 until the opening of their new Chamber in 1950 the Commons sat in the Lords' Chamber. The Woolsack was removed and a temporary Speaker's Chair was placed at the opposite end of the Chamber. In 1951 the Chamber was thoroughly renovated, the standing brass candelabra were brought back, and hanging chandeliers of a new design were installed with the object of revealing the original splendour of Pugin's decorations. At the same time the space behind the Bar was enlarged so as to give more room for Counsel when pleading in Appeals and to provide seats for distinguished visitors. The Lords returned to their Chamber on 29 May 1951.

The Peers' Lobby

The Peers' Lobby is 38 ft (11.5 m) square and 33 ft (10 m) high. There are four doorways: the north leading to the Central Lobby, the south into the Chamber, the east to the House of Lords Library and Peers' Dining Room, and the west to the Moses Room and offices of the House of Lords. Above each arch is a series of six panels on which are painted the arms of the royal lines of England – Saxon, Norman, Plantagenet, Tudor, Stuart and Brunswick (i.e. Hanoverian) – with the initial letter of each carved below. Over the east and west doors are the arms of Scotland, England and Ireland; over the south door are the royal arms and motto.

The solid brass gates leading into the Chamber, decorated with roses, thistles and shamrocks, and the centre-piece of fine enamel inlaid with brass in the floor were made by John Hardman & Son, of Birmingham. The encaustic tiling of the floor was made by Minton of Staffordshire; the marble is from Derbyshire. The stained glass windows, which display the arms of noble families, were destroyed in the Second World War and have been restored. The ceiling was recently substantially restored.

The Moses Room

To the west of the Peers' Lobby lies a large room at the disposal of the Chairman of Committees, known as the Moses Room from the large fresco of *Moses bringing down the Tables of the Law from Mount Sinai*. This picture by J. R. Herbert, R.A., was completed in 1864, and like some other fresco paintings in the building had to be specially treated. The other picture in the room, *The Judgment of Daniel*, by the same artist, is painted in oil on canvas and was hung in 1880. It was originally intended to have a series of eight frescoes in the room illustrating the idea of Justice on Earth and its development in Law and Judgment.

The Library of the House of Lords

The House of Lords possessed no library until 1826, when Sir John Soane completed a substantial room south of the Painted Chamber. In the fire of 1834 the Library rooms were 'completely destroyed and gutted of every particle and timber', but almost all the books were saved. The volumes were passed along a line of soldiers to St Margaret's Church, where they were stacked together with those saved from the Commons Library. Temporary premises were provided until 1848, when the four beautiful rooms designed by Barry were occupied. Above the shelves are panels of the armorial bearings of the Chief Justices of England.

The major part of the collection of around 120,000 volumes is of legal and parliamentary works, but it is by no means confined to these subjects. It has a substantial reference collection, and equipment for providing access to current information systems, while preserving a fine historical collection.

The House of Lords Record Office

The records of Parliament are in the charge of the House of Lords Record Office and are housed in the Victoria Tower (*see* p. 30). These records may be consulted by members of the public between the hours of 9.30 a.m. and 5 p.m., Mondays to Fridays, on application to the Clerk of the Records. Those visiting the Record Office should approach by the Chancellor's Gate.

The repository in the Tower was completely reconstructed between 1948 and 1963. It consists of twelve air-conditioned floors with a total area of some 32,400 sq ft (3,010 sq m) and contains about 5½ miles (8.8 km) of steel shelves for the documents. The Record Office has custody of such historic manuscripts as the Attainder of Catherine Howard, the record of the Trial of Mary Queen of Scots, the original Bill of Rights, and documents signed by Queen Elizabeth I, Oliver Cromwell, Samuel Pepys, Sir Christopher Wren and Lord Nelson. A small permanent display of historic documents is situated in the Royal Gallery (*see* p. 35).

The archives in the Victoria Tower include the master copies of all Acts of Parliament since 1497, endorsed in Norman French, the Journals, Minutes, Petitions, Papers and other official records of the two Houses, together with the archives of the Lord Great Chamberlain and historical documents presented to either House or bought by them, including modern political papers, such as the Lloyd George papers. Until 1497 the Clerks of the Parliaments, who were also Chancery clerks, took their records back with them into Chancery at the end of a session. Mediaeval parliamentary records are thus now to be found principally amongst the Chancery Proceedings in the Public Record Office, Chancery Lane. The House of Lords MSS form one of the principal sources for modern British history, and have been used by many historians from Lord Macaulay onwards.

The Peers' Corridor

Leading from the Peers' Lobby to the Central Lobby is the Peers' Corridor adorned with pictures of the Stuart period by C. W. Cope, R.A. completed between 1856 and 1866, some in fresco and some in water-glass. Those on the east side were intended to illustrate aspects of the virtues and heroism of Parliamentarians: those on the west, of Royalists. Sketches for some of these are displayed on the walls of the staircase leading down to the Barry Room (*see* p. 45).

On the east side, from the Peers' Lobby:

1. Lord Russell taking leave of his wife before going to his execution for complicity in the Rye House plot, 1683.

2. The embarkation of the Pilgrim Fathers from Delft Haven in 1620.

3. The Train Bands leaving London to relieve the siege of Gloucester, 1643.

4. Speaker Lenthall asserting the privileges of the House of Commons when Charles I came to arrest the Five Members, 4 January 1642.

On the west side, from the Central Lobby:

5. Charles I raising his standard at Nottingham, 22 August 1642.

6. Basing House, the seat of the Marquess of Winchester, defended against the Parliamentary army.

7. The expulsion of the Fellows of Oxford colleges for refusing to sign the Covenant to extirpate Popery in 1648.

8. The burial of Charles I at St George's Chapel, Windsor in a snowstorm on 9 February 1649, with Colonel Whichcot, the Governor of Windsor Castle, refusing to allow Bishop Juxon to read from the Book of Common Prayer.

The windows above, showing the arms of Richard II, Henry IV, Henry V and Henry VI, were designed by Pugin and executed by Hardman, originally in bright colours, but, following complaints, remade in gold and silver grisaille.

Lords' Refreshment Rooms

The Peers' Guest Room, which is between the Lords' Library and the Pugin Room, is hung with pictures, including Sir Edwin Landseer's *Duke of Wellington showing the battlefield of Waterloo to his daughter-in-law, the Marchioness of Douro*, and J. R. Herbert's *Acquittal of the Seven Bishops*. The Peers' Dining Room was originally to have been decorated with panels illustrating hunting scenes, including Sir Edwin Landseer's *Monarch of the Glen*; but the plan was abandoned in 1850. The original model for a window in the Chamber of the House of Lords showing William the Conqueror was placed here in 1988; there are also several paintings of the House of Lords in session between 1829 and 1851. In June 1989 the Barry Room, on the ground floor, was opened as a dining room for Peers and their guests.

12   The Central Lobby of the House of Commons

The House of Commons

The Central Lobby

The Central Lobby is the place where visitors and constituents, coming to see Members of Parliament, may fill in their names on green cards, send them in to Members and await their arrival.

It is an octagonal apartment, 75 ft (22.8 m) high and 60 ft (18.2 m) across, with a vaulted stone roof. Above is the central tower of the Palace 300 ft (91.4 m) high. The roof contains upwards of 50 elaborate carved bosses, the panels between the ribs being filled with mosaics. Four arched doorways, with statues of kings and queens on either side, four arched windows of modern tinted glass, and four large mosaic panels above the doorways are the chief features of the Lobby. The west doorway leads to St Stephen's Hall, the south to the House of Lords, the north to the House of Commons, the east to the dining rooms and libraries. In January 1943 the vault beneath the Lobby was equipped with machine tools, and until 1945 a team of part-time workers drawn from Members, officials and others connected with the Palace made precision instruments for the Ministry of Supply. The space is now occupied in part by a staff bar.

The mosaic panel over the south door, representing St George, was designed by Sir Edward Poynter, and unveiled in 1870. St George, the patron saint of England and of the Order of the Garter, has the dragon at his feet; on his right is a figure symbolizing Fortitude, carrying St George's banner in her left hand and a club in her right hand; on his left is a figure symbolizing Purity, bearing St George's helmet and a bunch of white lilies. The panel over the north door, representing St David, was also designed by Sir Edward Poynter and completed in 1898. The saint is shown carrying the bishop's cross, with the dove alighting on his shoulder and two angels as supporters, one carrying the harp and the other a lamp, symbolizing Harmony and Light. Both these works were executed in Venice by Salviati, working for the Venice and Murano Glass Company, and were paid for from public funds.

The panel over the east door, which depicts St Andrew, was presented by Sir William Raeburn, M.P. It was designed by R. Anning Bell, R.A., executed *in situ*, and unveiled in 1923. St Andrew, the fisherman, stands in the centre, holding his staff and net, with the diagonal cross behind him. St Margaret, Queen of Scotland, on his left, carries the Bible and a black cross, known as the Holy Rood of Scotland, containing in a central reliquary a portion of the True Cross, given to her ancestor by Charlemagne. On his right stands St Mungo (known also as St Kentigern), the founder of the See of Glasgow, with a bishop's mitre and crozier, and at his feet a salmon with a ring in its mouth. Above is the monogram of Christ with the Alpha and Omega, the ancient Christian symbol which is found on two of the earliest tombs in Scotland. The panel over the west door representing St Patrick, which was presented by Sir Patrick Ford, M.P., was also designed by R. Anning Bell, executed *in situ*, and unveiled in 1924. St Patrick stands with clasped hands, clad in the robes of a bishop, with the Rock of Cashel behind him, on which is engraved the word Banba, the Erse name for Ireland, and the shamrock at his feet. On his right is St Columba, representing the North of Ireland, with a shield at his feet, on which is the Red Hand of Ulster; on his left is St Bridget with the Irish Harp at her feet.

There are four large marble statues: of Earl Russell and the Earl of Iddesleigh by Sir Edgar Boehm; of Earl Granville by Hamo Thornycroft; and of Gladstone by F. W. Pomeroy. The encaustic tiling on the floor, a masterpiece designed by Pugin and executed by Minton, contains in Latin the sentence 'Except the Lord build the house, their labour is but lost that build it. Psalm cxxvii.' Adjoining the entrance to the Strangers' Gallery may be seen a portion of the grille removed from the Ladies' Gallery on 23 August 1917. The great central chandelier dates from 1854 and was made by Hardman to Pugin's design.

The Commons Corridor

This corridor is adorned by eight pictures by E. M. Ward, R.A., of historic incidents of the Stuart period, completed between 1857 and 1868.

Those on the east side relate to 1650–60:

1. Charles II escaping after the battle of Worcester to Bristol, disguised as the servant of Jane Lane.

2. Montrose led to execution on 21 May 1650 having Wishart's book tied round his neck by the executioner. (He said he was prouder of that decoration than of the Order of the Garter.)

3. Charles II landing at Dover, 26 May 1660 (note the anachronism of the Union Jack in the lower right-hand corner).

4. General Monck declaring for a free Parliament, 1659.

Those on the west side relate to 1685–89:

5. Alice Lisle concealing fugitives after the battle of Sedgemoor, 1685, where the Duke of Monmouth was defeated; she was condemned to death by Judge Jeffreys.

6. The last sleep of Argyll, showing his peaceful sleep before his execution on 30 June 1685 for attempting to free Scotland from James II.

7. Parliament offering the Crown to William and Mary in the Banqueting Hall at Whitehall, 13 February 1689.

8. The acquittal of the Seven Bishops who were tried in Westminster Hall for refusing to read James II's Declaration of Indulgence, 30 June 1688.

The windows in gold and silver grisaille (*see* Peers' Corridor, p. 45) show the arms of a number of royal princes of the fifteenth century, together with heraldic supporters.

The Members' Lobby

The Commons, or Members', Lobby is about 45 ft (13.7 m) square with four arched doorways, one leading into the Chamber, another leading to the Members' Entrance, the third to the Central Lobby, and the fourth to the libraries, dining rooms and terrace. This part of the building was seriously damaged by the air raid of 10 May 1941 and was rebuilt in a simplified version of the nineteenth-century style (*see* p. 27–8).

At Winston Churchill's suggestion the archway into the Chamber was rebuilt from the damaged stonework of the original arch, which is thus preserved 'as a monument to the ordeal', which Westminster endured in the Second World War and as 'a reminder to those who will come centuries after us, that they may look back from time to time upon their forebears who "kept the bridge in the brave days of old".'

On the left of the arch is a bronze statue of Sir Winston Churchill by Oscar Nemon, unveiled in 1969; on the right is a statue of David Lloyd George by Uli Nimptsch. The other four statues, all of prime ministers, are of Benjamin Disraeli by Count Gleichen (formerly in the Upper Waiting Hall), Arthur Balfour by David McFall, Herbert Asquith by Leonard Merrifield and Gilbert Bayes, and Clement Attlee by Ivor Roberts-Jones, unveiled on 12 November 1979. To the left of the entrance from the Commons Corridor is a bust of James Ramsay Macdonald by Jacob Epstein, given by his family in 1989.

In the doorkeeper's chair on the right hand of the arch is the lever used for setting the division bells ringing when a vote is called (*see* p. 53). Here, too, is kept a snuff-box traditionally provided for the use of Members. The box now in use is made of oak taken from the bombed Chamber. Next to the statue of Lloyd George are the windows of the Vote Office, which supplies Members with parliamentary papers and other official publications. There are two message boards in the Lobby; when there is an urgent message or note for a Member, his or her name is automatically illuminated.

On the west side of the Lobby is the Members' Post Office, part of a complex operation (dating back to 1698) for the sorting and delivery of Members' mail; Members are entitled to free postage. To the south-west and south-east are the offices of the Government and Opposition Whips.

The Chamber of the House of Commons

The Chamber which the Commons had occupied since 1852 was entirely destroyed by fire in the air raid on the night of 10 May 1941. The Commons then moved into the House of Lords Chamber, where they remained until the end of July 1950.

The floor of the present Chamber is exactly the same size as that of the old, that is, 68 ft (20.7 m) by 45½ ft (13.8 m), but above the gallery level its dimensions were increased from 46½ ft (14.1 m) by 84 ft (25.6 m to 48 ft (14.6 m) by 103 ft (31.3 m), to provide 171 more seats for strangers and reporters. There are 929 seats (including those behind the stone screens) of which 427 are for Members, 326 for strangers, 161 for reporters, and 15 for officials. The total height of the Chamber is 46 ft (14 m) as compared with 44 ft (13.4 m) formerly.

The new Chamber was designed by Sir Giles Gilbert Scott, in a style designed to be in keeping with the rest of the Palace, which could broadly be designated as late Gothic; but no attempt was made to follow the design of the old stonework or woodwork. A domestic type of window was adopted as being more suitable than the somewhat ecclesiastical type in the old Chamber. The general characteristic of the oak work is a concentration of ornament in horizontal bands with contrasting plain areas. The oak, which grew in Shropshire, was treated with iron sulphate to make it a light grey. The new buildings were faced, internally and externally, with a variety of stones, the principal being Clipsham quarried in Rutland.

The Chamber originally built by Barry for the Commons was of similar design to the Lords' Chamber, although less ornate. When they first occupied it in 1850, Members complained of poor audibility and insisted that the flat ceiling should be redesigned to rise from the sides towards the centre. The ceiling of the present Chamber retains this general shape. Until 1991, the Chamber was lit exclusively by fluorescent lighting from behind glass ceiling panels. Since October 1991, and following extensive trials with prototypes, six hexagonal lanterns with tubular strip-lights behind opaque glass panels have been used, designed to provide sufficient lighting for television cameras. Only the west windows admit natural light; automatic blinds are used to protect the Chamber from too strong an afternoon light.

The benches, in the backs of which are sound amplifiers, are upholstered in green hide, and the floor is covered with a mottled green carpet. The red stripes that run the length of the front benches are traditionally two swords' length apart; and Members speaking from the front bench must not step over them.

The furniture was given by the then members of the British Commonwealth of Nations; the Speaker's Chair by Australia, the Table by Canada, the despatch boxes by New Zealand, the three Clerks' chairs by South Africa, the Serjeant at Arms' chair by Ceylon, the entrance doors by India and Pakistan, the Bar of the House by Jamaica, and the furniture

13 The House of Commons in session, awaiting Black Rod's summons to
the House of Lords to hear the Queen's Speech, 6 May 1992

in the Division Lobbies by Nigeria and Uganda. (*see* Appendix). Two
electronic digital clocks were fitted in 1977.

The 19 Members who lost their lives in the First World War are
commemorated by the shields beneath the South Gallery, which are
emblazoned with their arms and initials. Similar shields, beneath the
North Gallery, commemorate the 23 Members who died in the Second
World War. The central shield beneath the South Gallery was painted
with the arms of Airey Neave, M.P., following his assassination in 1979.

In the south-west corner of the Chamber, under the Gallery, is the
commentary box constructed in 1976 for the purpose of radio
broadcasting of the House's proceedings. Proceedings were first broadcast
on an experimental basis in June 1975, and on 3 April 1978 a permanent

system of sound broadcasting was inaugurated. Since 1966 the House periodically rejected the idea of televising its proceedings. On 9 February 1988 the House approved in principle the holding of an experiment in the public broadcasting of its proceedings by television. On 19 July 1990 the House approved televising on a permanent basis. The pictures are taken by eight remote-control cameras, operated by CCT Productions Ltd under contract; the footage is made available to broadcasters.

The Speaker's Chair designed by Pugin, which had been used since 1852, was destroyed when the House of Commons was bombed. The Chairs in use before 1834 were copies of that designed by Wren in 1706. Before 1834 the Speaker was entitled to take away his Chair as a perquisite on retirement. The Chair of Sir Fletcher Norton, Speaker 1769–80, may be seen in the Museum of London. The Chair used by Speaker Abbot from 1802 to 1817 is in the possession of All Souls College, Oxford. The oldest relic of a Speaker's Chair survives in Radley Church in Oxfordshire – the canopy of the Chair occupied by Speaker Lenthall from 1640 until 1653, when he was dragged from it by Cromwell's musketeers on the dispersal of the Long Parliament. A temporary Chair was used from 1941 to 1951 while the Commons sat in the Lords' Chamber. The present Chair was given by Australia and is made of black bean from Northern Queensland. At the back of the Chair hangs the bag in which Members deposit petitions presented to the House on behalf of members of the public or outside organizations. Exact replicas of the Pugin Chair were presented by the Commonwealth Parliamentary Association (United Kingdom Branch) to the House of Commons in Canada and to the House of Representatives in Australia, and in both cases portions of old oak from the roof of Westminster Hall and from Nelson's flagship *Victory* were incorporated. Specially designed Speaker's Chairs have traditionally been given to Commonwealth countries on their achievement of independence.

The Division Lobbies are at each side of the Chamber. Members voting 'Aye' go out of the Chamber behind the Speaker's Chair, and pass through the Lobby on the Speaker's right. Those voting 'No' go out at the other end of the Chamber into the Lobby on the Speaker's left. At the farther end of each Lobby, Clerks record the names of Members and a pair of Members, 'Tellers', count them. Members are summoned to vote in divisions by bells which ring in all parts of the building occupied by the Commons except the Committee Rooms, where divisions are called by the policeman on duty, in the outlying parliamentary precincts and in

14 Sir Charles Barry, by J. H. Foley

ministries and other offices around Westminster. Members have eight minutes in which to enter one or other of the Lobbies, after which the doors are locked.

In the 'No' Lobby are displayed originals and reproductions of the original manuscript Commons Journals, showing such entries as those of 18 January 1621, where James I tore out the Commons' Protestation of their rights and privileges; 4 January 1642, the record of the attempted arrest of the Five Members by Charles I; 20 April 1653, the record of Cromwell expelling the Rump Parliament; Queen Elizabeth I's rebuke to the Commons on 24 January 1581; the discovery of the Gunpowder Plot in 1605; and the Declaration of Rights of 12 February 1689.

The Library of the House of Commons

In 1800 a house in Abingdon Street was built for the use of the Clerk of the Journals, and it was here that the Library of the House of Commons was first formed. Until 1818 it consisted of the Journals of the House and official papers only. In that year it was decided that books other than official papers likely to be useful to Members should occasionally be bought and, to house them, a room 17 ft (5.1 m) square was provided within the Palace. In the same year the first Librarian was appointed. In 1827 three rooms were provided and the Library received its first vote, a sum of £2,000, with which to expand. This process was almost complete when the fire of 1834 destroyed two-thirds of the contents of the Library. A temporary home was used until 1852, when Sir Charles Barry provided the existing range of five large rooms on the Terrace front. A sixth room, which previously formed part of the Speaker's residence, was allocated to the use of the Library in 1966. There is also a branch library for the use of Members and their staff at 1 Derby Gate, together with an extensive Research Division.

The Library provides a comprehensive research and reference service to Members. It also has a number of computer terminals to access its own database, POLIS, and several external databases. It takes some 2,000 newspapers and periodicals, and houses more than 150,000 bound books and a total of about 750,000 other documents and papers. A Public Information Office publishes a weekly information bulletin and a series of factsheets, as well as answering inquiries from the public about the work of the House. Apart from these services, the Library and its facilities are exclusively for Members.

In the Oriel Room is a bust, by Alexander Ritchie, of Joseph Hume (1777–1855) the leader of the Radical party and the tireless champion of every kind of reform, especially in finance; it has been said that when he died he had served on more committees and had made more, longer and probably worse speeches than any other private Member. In Room C the space above the shelves is filled by a chronological list of the Speakers from 1377. At the end of the room is a bust, by Bruce-Joy, of Lord Farnborough, better known as Thomas Erskine May (1815–86), who served both as Assistant Librarian and Clerk of the House of Commons. Successive editions of his *Parliamentary Practice* have been the prime authority on the procedure of the House since 1844.

The Smoking, Chess and Refreshment Rooms

Next to the Library on the river front is the Members' Smoking Room, a comfortably furnished room with oak panelling. The ceiling has recently been returned to its original decorative treatment. The pictures include portraits of Charles James Fox and Edmund Burke, after Sir Joshua Reynolds.

Next to the Smoking Room is the Chess Room, where Members can indulge in chess and, since 1987, other board and card games. A handsome set of carved ivory chessmen was presented by Mr Arthur Walter in memory of the Westminster *v* Washington chess match in 1897, when the House of Commons played the House of Representatives of the United States by cable.

The Members' Dining Room is next to the Chess Room. Among the pictures are a painting of the House of Commons in session about 1715, by Peter Tillemans, and portraits of the younger Pitt, Speaker Onslow, Luke Hansard, Sir Robert Walpole, Gladstone and Disraeli. The ceilings of the two originally separate rooms now joined as one have both been returned to their original states.

Next to the Members' Dining Room is the Strangers' Dining Room to which Members may introduce strangers. In addition to the pictures of several former Speakers and politicians is the official portrait, by June Mendoza, of the House in session in July 1986, completed in October 1987, and showing over 400 Members and staff; and a picture by Andrew Festing commissioned by 156 Members not included in that portrait and showing them in seven scenes set in the Smoking Room and Library.

Adjoining this is the Members' Guest Room, renamed the Pugin Room and restored in 1978. Here hang portraits of Augustus Welby Pugin by J. R. Herbert, of his third wife Jane, and of Charles Barry by H. W. Pickersgill. In the oriel window are the mallet and chisels used on the

15 Augustus Welby Pugin, by J. R. Herbert

building of the Palace of Westminster by Henry Broadhurst, stone-mason (who afterwards became a Member of Parliament from 1880 to 1906), and similar tools used in the reconstruction of the Chamber of the House of Commons after its destruction in 1941.

There is also a Members' Tea Room where Members may read the national and the chief provincial daily papers, the weekly press and some overseas papers.

Before 1773 no food could be obtained in the building, but in that year John Bellamy was permitted to open a small room to supply provisions for consumption on the premises. Lord Rosebery, in one of the appendices of his *Life of William Pitt*, quotes a story told at first hand to Disraeli that Pitt's last words were: 'I think I could eat one of Bellamy's veal pies.' Since 1773, food has been obtainable at any time during the sittings of the House. From 1848 to 1978 its supply was in the hands of a Select Committee, since 1965 the Catering Sub-Committee of the Select Committee of the House of Commons (Services). It is now the responsibility of a separately constituted Refreshment Department. It has been ruled that in the sale of liquor in the precincts of the House without a licence, the House is acting in a matter which falls within the privileges of the House, so that no court of law has jurisdiction to interfere. (*Rex* v *Sir R. F. Graham-Campbell*, ex parte *Herbert*, (1935) 1K.B. 595.)

The East Corridor

The six frescoes in this corridor were placed in position in 1910, under the artistic supervision of Edwin Abbey, and depict episodes of the Tudor period. The subjects are, from the south-west corner:

1. St Thomas More and Erasmus visiting the children of Henry VII at Greenwich in 1499, painted by Frank Cadogan Cowper, and presented by the Earl of Carlisle: above are paintings by Cowper showing Edward IV and Richard III.

2. John Cabot, the discoverer of Newfoundland, receiving a charter from Henry VII in 1496 to search for new lands, painted by Denis Eden and presented by Lord Winterstoke.

3. The origin of the badges of Lancaster and York, Richard Plantagenet plucking a white rose for the Yorkists and the Earl of Somerset a red rose for Lancaster in the Temple Gardens, painted by Henry Payne and presented by the Earl of Beauchamp.

4. The entry of Queen Mary and Princess Elizabeth into London after the death of Edward VI, 1553, painted by Byam Shaw and presented by Lord Airedale.

5. Latimer preaching before Edward VI at St Paul's Cross in 1548, painted by Ernest Board and presented by Lord Wandsworth.

6. Henry VIII and Catherine of Aragon appearing before Cardinal Wolsey and the Papal Legate at Blackfriars in 1529, painted by Frank Salisbury and presented by Lord Stanmore.

Lower Waiting Hall

The Lower Waiting Hall is chiefly used as a passage to the dining and smoking rooms, and a stone staircase leads up to the Committee Rooms. Here are: a marble bust of Oliver Cromwell, wrongly ascribed to Bernini, and probably of eighteenth-century workmanship; busts of Keir Hardie by Benno Schotz, Ernest Bevin by Jacob Epstein, on loan from the Tate Gallery, and R. A. Butler by Angela Conner, presented by his family in 1991; statues of John Bright, by Albert Bruce-Joy, and of Sir William Harcourt, by Waldo Story; and the Book of Remembrance, which records the names of Members and servants of the House of Commons, and of sons and daughters of Members of the wartime House, who were killed in the Second World War. Just off the Hall is a lounge for the use of Members' families.

Committee Staircase

At the bottom of the Committee staircase is a statue of Sir Charles Barry, shown examining the ground plan of the Palace and the plans for the Victoria Tower, by J. H. Foley, R.A. On the stair are marble busts of six prime ministers: the younger Pitt, Spencer Perceval, George Canning, Sir Robert Peel, Palmerston and Gladstone. On the stair landing is a picture of the Commons petitioning Queen Elizabeth to marry, by Solomon J. Solomon, R.A., presented by Lord Swaythling in 1912. It includes several portraits of celebrities of that date, including Lord Swaythling himself, Speaker Lowther, John Burns, Lewis Harcourt and Sir Courtenay Ilbert. The staircase contains the most accessible series of stained glass windows designed by Pugin and executed by Hardman, celebrating Edward, Prince of Wales, the Black Prince, eldest son of Edward III and showing the honours, titles, badges, coats of arms, etc., associated with the Prince and his contemporaries. Built into the wall on the right-hand side of the stair are the standard yard measure and one pound weight deposited for testing purposes.

16 The Upper Waiting, or Poets', Hall

Upper Waiting Hall

The Upper Waiting Hall, at the top of the staircase leading to the Committee Rooms, was called the Poets' Hall, from the fresco paintings with which the panels were decorated. The frescoes, which illustrated scenes from English poetry, were completed in 1854 but quickly deteriorated and were covered up for many years. They have been recently uncovered, conserved and splendidly restored. Clockwise from the north-west corner they represent:

1. Griselda's first Trial of Patience – the Marquis causes her child to be taken from her, from Chaucer's *Canterbury Tales*, by C. W. Cope.

2. The Red Cross Knight overcoming the Dragon, from Spenser's *Faerie Queene*, by G. F. Watts.

3. King Lear disinheriting Cordelia, from Shakespeare's *King Lear*, by J. R. Herbert.

4. Satan touched by Ithuriel's spear while whispering evil dreams into the ear of Eve, from Milton's *Paradise Lost*, by J. C. Horsley.

5. St Cecilia, from Dryden's *Song for St Cecilia's Day*, by John Tenniel.

6. Personification of the Thames and of the English rivers, from Pope's *Windsor Forest*, by Edward Armitage.

7. Death of Marmion, from Scott's *Marmion*, by Edward Armitage.

8. Death of Lara, from Byron's *Lara*, by C. W. Cope.

The eight statues on the plinths come from the exterior of the building and were removed during restorations. The statue of Joseph Chamberlain (with an orchid in his buttonhole) by John Tweed was formerly in the Members' Lobby and exchanged places with that of Benjamin Disraeli in 1990.

Terrace Staircase

On the walls of the staircase and the lobby leading to the Terrace are hung Professor Tristram's reconstructions (painted in the 1930s) of some of the paintings which adorned the Palace before the fire of 1834. At the top of the stairs is the coronation of Edward the Confessor, the original of which was in the Painted Chamber, dated about 1270. Lining the stairs and above them are scenes from the Book of Maccabees, also from the Painted Chamber; those in the lobby at the foot of the stairs are from St Stephen's Chapel (*see* p. 8). In the lobby is the original hammer of Big Ben (*see* p. 26). A lion and unicorn, removed from the exterior during stone replacement, flank the door to the Terrace.

Terrace Floor

On the Terrace floor to the north are a Strangers' Cafeteria, Members' Cafeteria, and the Strangers' Bar, opposite which is a bust of John Redmond by E. W. Doyle Jones. South of these are several private dining rooms, and the Churchill (formerly Harcourt) Room, used as a Grill Room, and containing a series of coloured lithographs of the 1851 Great

Exhibition and a painting of Venice by Sir Winston Churchill, given by Lady Churchill. During the summer months, tents are erected on the Terrace and refreshments served.

In the Terrace corridor hangs a glass case containing specimens of the tally-sticks used to receive payments into the Exchequer, the burning of which caused the fire of 1834 (*see* p. 15). Another case contains one of the original annunciators installed in 1891 to indicate the business in progress in the Commons Chamber and the name of the Member speaking. In 1968 these machines were replaced by closed-circuit television annunciators, of which around 1,500 are now in use in Ministers' and Members' rooms and all public rooms. It is proposed to replace these by a dual data and video network. A similar system was installed in the House of Lords in 1973.

A third case contains the letters patent of Mr Speaker Shaw-Lefevre, created Viscount Eversley in 1857, with the Great Seal of Queen Victoria appended. Nearby hangs a collection of service and civilian medals, including the Albert Medal awarded in 1885 to Police Constable William Cole for gallantry in saving Westminster Hall from the effects of a Fenian bomb. In the corridor are some pictures of the destruction of the old Palace and a copy of the painting by Charles Sims of the introduction of Viscountess Astor by Mr Lloyd George and Mr Balfour to the House of Commons in 1919. The original was hung on the Committee Stairs in 1924 but removed after protests from Members who resented the portrait of a living politician being hung in the Palace. A rule was made in 1925 that no portrait, bust or other representation of any living person or any person deceased less than ten years should be exhibited within the precincts except in very exceptional circumstances (but *see* p. 29).

Committee Rooms

On the first floor overlooking the river there are the Committee and Private Bill Office and sixteen Committee Rooms of both Houses of varying capacity, some (Nos. 10 and 14), holding as many as 150 people, others (Nos. 7 and 13), holding only 30 people. Two modern Committee Rooms have also been provided at the south end of the corridor, overlooking Peers' Court, and five on the Upper Committee Corridor. Many committee meetings are open to the public. A weekly list of these meetings is posted outside St Stephen's Entrance. In the Committee Rooms are a number of pictures of historic subjects, including: in No. 2, three paintings by Benjamin West relating to *Edward III and the Order of the Garter*, lent by H.M. The Queen; in No. 4, *The Coronation of George V*, by J. H. F. Bacon and *The Coronation of George VI*, by Frank Salisbury; in No. 7, *Henry VIII and Cardinal Wolsey*, by Sir John Gilbert; in No. 10, *Alfred inciting the Saxons to repel the Danes*, by G. F. Watts, and *The Burial of the Unknown Warrior in Westminster Abbey*, by Frank Salisbury; in No. 11, *The Speaker's Procession in 1884*, by F. W. Lawson; in No. 13, *The Field of the Cloth of Gold*, by Sir John Gilbert; in No. 14, several pictures illustrative of the Civil War period, including *The Flight of the Five Members*, by Seymour Lucas, and *Mr Speaker Finch held down in the Chair, March 2, 1629*, by A. C. Gow.

Some Committee Rooms, and a number of other rooms throughout the Palace, are decorated with wallpapers printed from the original wood blocks that were cut to patterns designed by Pugin.

The pictures hung in the Committee corridor include a fine collection of portraits on loan from the National Portrait Gallery; outside Room 8 are some studies for the series of wall paintings, *The Building of Britain*, in St Stephen's Hall (*see* p. 10). Outside Room 14 is a bronze bust of Oliver Cromwell after Edward Pierce's posthumous marble bust. In the corridor opposite Room 13 is a bust of Charles Stewart Parnell and a painting of *The men who made Home Rule* [for Ireland].

17 Madam Speaker, accompanied by Black Rod, leads the House of Commons to the House of Lords to hear the Queen's Speech

Parliament: its Composition, Procedure and Ceremonial

The Composition of Parliament

Parliament consists of the Sovereign, the House of Lords and the House of Commons, and every bill (with certain exceptions under the Parliament Acts 1911 and 1949) before it becomes an Act of Parliament has to pass through both Houses and receive the Royal Assent. The enacting words of every Act are: 'Be it enacted by the Queen's most Excellent Majesty, by and with the advice and consent of the Lords Spiritual and Temporal, and Commons, in this present Parliament assembled and by the authority of the same, as follows.'

House of Lords

The House of Lords comprises the Lords Spiritual and Temporal. The Lords Spiritual are the 2 Archbishops and 24 senior diocesan Bishops of the Church of England. In May 1993, there were 1,186 Lords Temporal, 82 of whom were without writs of summons (hereditary peers who have not expressed a wish to sit in the House of Lords), and 89 of whom were on leave of absence (granted on request to those who wish to record inability to attend for the remainder of a Parliament). They comprised:

1. 776 hereditary peers of England, Scotland, Great Britain and the United Kingdom (of whom 17 were peers of first creation and 17 were hereditary peeresses in their own right);

2. 19 life peers created under the Appellate Jurisdiction Act 1876 and subsequent enactments to carry out the judicial functions of the House as Lords of Appeal in Ordinary; and

3. 391 life peers created under the Life Peerages Act 1958 (of whom 59 were women).

Edward I summoned 140 lords to the so-called Model Parliament of 1295: 2 archbishops and 19 bishops; 70 abbots and priors; 8 earls and 41 barons. At the time of the Revolution of 1688 the House consisted of 150 lay and 24 spiritual lords. From 1714 to 1760 the total membership was about 220, but mainly as a consequence of the many creations of George III this figure had risen to about 400 in 1830. By the end of the century the House numbered 591.

The Life Peerages Act 1958 made possible the appointment of peers for life. Such peers could be of either sex; and this was the first time that women were admitted as Members of the House of Lords. The Peerage Act 1963: (1) authorized the disclaimer for life of hereditary peerages; (2) abolished the system of Scottish representative peers provided by the Treaty of Union and admitted all Scottish peers to the House of Lords; (3) gave to women holders of hereditary peerages the right to sit and vote in the House; (4) permitted Irish peers to be elected as Members of the House of Commons for any constituency in the United Kingdom. Since the death in 1961 of the last of the Irish representative peers provided by the Act of Union no one has sat in the House of Lords in virtue of an Irish peerage.

Members of the House of Lords are unpaid; but since 1946 have been entitled to recover travelling expenses incurred when attending the House. Since 1957 certain other expenses have also been recoverable. In January 1993 the expense allowances were up to £69 for overnight accommodation, and up to £31 for day subsistence, as well as incidental travel costs and secretarial expenses.

House of Commons

The House of Commons has since the Election of April 1992 consisted of 651 Members; 524 from England, 72 from Scotland, 38 from Wales, and 17 from Northern Ireland.

Edward I summoned to the Model Parliament 74 knights of the shire and 234 citizens and burgesses. The Act of Union with Scotland of 1707 increased the membership of the Commons House from 513 to 558, and the Act of Union with Ireland of 1800 added 100 Members, bringing the total up to 658. The Act of 1884 increased it to 670, and the Representation of the People Act 1918 increased it further to the highest figure at which it has ever stood – 707. The Irish Free State Act 1922 reduced the number of Irish Members from 105 to 13 representing Northern Ireland. Sixty women were elected in the General Election of April 1992. The first woman elected to the House of Commons was Countess de Markiewicz, on 14 December 1918, for the St Patrick's Division of Dublin representing Sinn Fein; as a protest, she did not take her seat. The first woman to take her seat was Viscountess Astor, elected for Plymouth, Sutton at a by-election on 15 November 1919. A limit of five years is set to the duration of a Parliament by the Parliament Act 1911.

In the Middle Ages Members were paid by their constituents, the amount being fixed at four shillings a day for knights of the shire and two shillings a day for burgesses. Although payments continued to be made voluntarily by some boroughs as late as the reign of Charles II, the practice became obsolete; in fact, the reverse process (namely, for the Member to pay his constituents heavily for their votes) became prevalent.

A salary was first paid to Members in 1911, when it was £400 a year. In January 1993 the basic salary was £30,854 a year. In addition Members are entitled to certain free travel concessions and a car mileage allowance, and to allowances in respect of secretarial and research assistance and the costs of staying away from their main residences in order to carry out their parliamentary duties. Ministers are paid a reduced parliamentary salary and a separate ministerial salary, producing a total salary of between £44,611 and £63,047, dependent on ministerial rank. The Prime Minister receives £76,234.

The payment of a separate salary to the Leader of the Opposition, a practice which originated in the Dominion of Canada in 1906, was adopted in the British House of Commons in 1937. Salaries are also now paid to the Leader of the Opposition and Chief Opposition Whip in the House of Lords and to the Chief Opposition Whip and one Assistant Opposition Whip in the Commons.

Sittings of the House of Commons

The sitting of the House each day is opened by the Speaker's procession. Preceded by a doorkeeper (wearing one of the royal messengers' badges

18 The Table of the House and the Speaker's Chair

dating from 1755) and the Serjeant at Arms, carrying the Mace, the Speaker is followed by the Train-bearer, Chaplain and Secretary. The Speaker's procession was probably instituted by Sir Thomas Gargrave in 1558. This procession passes through the Central Lobby and the Commons Lobby into the Chamber, the Mace is placed on the Table, the Speaker and Chaplain take their places at the Clerks' end of the Table, and the prayers are read by the Chaplain. After prayers the Speaker takes the Chair and the Chaplain bows himself out of the House.

When prayers are over, visitors holding tickets of admission may proceed from the Central Lobby to the galleries. The main public gallery faces the Speaker's Chair. On the floor of the House on the Speaker's right are the benches occupied by the supporters of the Government; the front bench is occupied by Ministers, the Prime Minister's seat being opposite the despatch box on the Table. On the Speaker's left is the Opposition side of the House, the Leader of the Opposition sitting opposite a despatch box on that side of the Table. Above the Speaker's Chair is the Reporters' Gallery; and under that gallery, to the Speaker's right, is the box for officials advising Ministers in the House.

On entering the gallery the visitor is given a copy of the Order Paper, which gives the agenda for the current day. The first item will probably be marked 'Private Business after Prayers' and refers solely to Private Bills. The proceedings on these bills are usually formal and brief.

Next, except on Friday, come 'Questions for Oral Answer'. The Speaker calls the name of the Member asking the first Question, the order of which has been previously established by a process of random selection. The Member rises and says, 'No. 1, Sir'. The Minister replies, after which the Member normally asks a supplementary Question arising from the answer. The Minister answers that, and other Members may then be called by the Speaker to ask supplementary Questions. Then the Speaker calls the next Question, and so on. The Questions on the paper must end by 3.30 p.m. Questions may then be asked which have not appeared on the Notice Paper, but which have been adjudged by the Speaker to be of an urgent character, and to relate either to matters of public importance or to the arrangement of business.

After Questions, Ministerial Statements may be made and applications made for emergency debates. The next item on the paper, entitled 'At the commencement of Public Business', consists of formal business such as Presentation of Bills and of Motions connected with the business of the House. The House now enters upon the main business, the 'Orders of the Day and Notices of Motions', which comprise the items on which debate takes place, namely, stages of Public Bills, and Government, Opposition or Private Members' motions. Twenty days are at the disposal of Opposition parties each session. Government Orders are marked with a star. Amendments to Bills of which notice has been given are printed as a separate paper.

The Orders of the Day are opened by the Speaker directing the Clerk to read the Orders of the Day. The Clerk rises and reads aloud the title of the Order, and the stage it is proposed to take. When a stage of a Bill is complete the House may either go on to a further stage of the same Bill or pass to the next Order on the paper and so on.

At the end of 'Orders of the Day and Notices of Motions' will be found a heading 'Questions for Written Answer'. Written answers are sent to the Members asking these Questions and are printed in the Official Report, as are written answers to Questions for Oral Answer not reached by 3.30 p.m.

At 10 p.m. on Mondays, Tuesdays, Wednesdays and Thursdays, and at 2.30 p.m. on Fridays, the proceedings on any business then under consideration are normally interrupted and a debate on a motion for the adjournment may then take place for half an hour. But certain kinds of business are exempted from interruption and the Government may seek to suspend the Standing Order which governs the sittings of the House to enable business to be taken after 10 p.m. In such cases the half-hour debate on the adjournment is taken after the exempted business. This half-hour at the end of the day's business gives a Member an opportunity to raise with a Minister a specific matter of policy or question of administration.

At the end of the sitting the Speaker does not walk in procession, but goes out behind the Chair, preceded by the Mace. The Parliamentary day ends with the cries of 'Who goes home?' and 'Usual time tomorrow' echoing through the lobbies, relics of the days when the streets were so unsafe that parties of Members going home in the same direction went together for safety, when there were no fixed hours for meeting and when, because printing was slow and copies scarce, Members were merely reminded orally of the time of meeting.

The first official photographs of the House of Commons in session were taken at the opening of Parliament on 21 April 1966, and the first photograph of the House in debate was taken during the debate on the Loyal Address in reply to the Queen's Speech on 12 November 1986. Photography is, as a rule, still not permitted, but clandestine photographs were taken by Mr Moore-Brabazon (then Member for Wallasey, later Lord Brabazon of Tara) during the debate on the Norwegian campaign, a few days before the destruction of the old Chamber on 10 May 1941. These are now preserved in the House of Lords Record Office. For television and radio, *see* pp. 52–3.

Sittings of the House of Lords

Sittings are presided over by the Lord Chancellor; the bishops sit immediately on his right hand, and the Government peers farther down the Chamber, with the Opposition parties on his left, and the peers unattached to a political party on the cross-benches facing him. During debates privy councillors (whether or not they are members of the House of Lords) and the eldest sons of peers may sit on the steps of the Throne. Although the Lord Chancellor presides, his position is unlike that of the Speaker in the Commons, as he lacks power to call members to order, and may himself participate in debate. However, the peers habitually respect their own conventions and Standing Orders, including one of 1626 against 'asperity of speech' which declares that 'it is for honour sake thought fit and so ordered, That all personal, sharp or taxing speeches be forborne'.

Procedure in the Lords is similar to that of the Commons, but simpler. After the arrival of the Lord Chancellor in procession, prayers are read by one of the bishops. There follow four oral questions to the Government, and then the House proceeds to the business of the day, whether legislation or debates. When the House goes into Committee, the Lord Chancellor leaves the Woolsack and the chair is taken by the Lord Chairman of Committees sitting at the Clerks' Table.

At a normal sitting, special costume is worn only by the Lord Chancellor and the bishops. However, parliamentary robes of scarlet and ermine are worn at the introduction of newly created peers, and all peers are robed when the Queen opens Parliament (*see* p. 74).

The House of Lords is also the final Court of Appeal for England, Wales and Northern Ireland, and in civil matters only, for Scotland. Judicial business is conducted by the Lords of Appeal, who are the Lord Chancellor, the Lords of Appeal in Ordinary, and such other peers as hold or have held high judicial office. Almost all Appeals are now heard by an Appellate Committee consisting of five Lords of Appeal sitting in a Committee Room. The members of the Committee subsequently meet in the House to deliver Judgment.

The Reporting of Debates

House of Lords

The earliest records of Parliament were of proceedings before the Lords. A contemporary picture of the Blackfriars Parliament of 1523 shows two parliamentary clerks kneeling behind a woolsack and making notes, presumably for later entry on the official Parliament Rolls, which had been kept since at least 1290. Petitions and Bills were carefully entered on the roll, but it is impossible to reconstruct a day to day chronicle from it. Unofficially, the clerks made fuller notes: the earliest record of a debate survives in the Clerk's notes of 1449, and the 'Fane Fragment' shows that journals were being kept by 1461. Seventeenth-century clerks sometimes recorded speeches in their 'scribbled books' and manuscript minutes; but these were highly confidential, and the Lords were at least as insistent as the Commons that debates must not be published. Many publishers and printers were hauled before them in the eighteenth century and cross-examined as to who supplied them with their copy; but, invariably they refused to divulge the names, and consequently were condemned to spend two or three weeks in the custody of Black Rod.

In spite of this, important debates were in fact published in summary form, and Cobbett in 1801 was able to add Lords' Debates to Commons' in his *Parliamentary History*. A special Gallery was provided for reporters in 1831, and in 1889 a table was set for them on the floor of the House between the opposing benches. Since 1917 the daily reports have been available the following morning. There is no verbatim report of judicial proceedings before the Appellate Committee. However, the Law Reports contain the full opinions of the Law Lords given on an Appeal and may provide notes on points of law arising in a case.

House of Commons

From early in the reign of Elizabeth I the House of Commons frowned upon the publication of its proceedings. In 1628 as a result of the King's expressing a desire to see a speech entered in the Journal, the House resolved that 'the entry of the clerk of particular men's speeches was without warrant at all times'. Nevertheless on 4 January 1642, when

Charles I came into the House of Commons to arrest the Five Members, the Clerk Assistant made shorthand notes of the King's speech, which was published by His Majesty's command. In the eighteenth century the House stiffened its resistance to the publication of its debates and twice – in 1738 and 1762 – declared such publication a breach of privilege. But it never succeeded in stopping the practice, and after about 1771 it was openly tolerated. The first continuous record of contemporary debates is that of Anchitell Grey, from 1667 to 1694, published as *Grey's Debates*.

Some of the records of debates from the earliest period to 1801 were collected by William Cobbett, and published under the title of *The Parliamentary History*. In 1803 the Press obtained a reserved portion of the Gallery for reporters, and Cobbett was responsible for the debates till 1812 when they passed into the hands of T. C. Hansard, who then gave his name to the Series. Charles Dickens made his debut as a reporter for *The Mirror of Parliament* in 1832 at the age of twenty. He has left an account of the Press Gallery in his *Sketches by Boz*.

Hansard's *Parliamentary Debates* were carried on under the original Hansard and his son, at first as a private individual, afterwards with a Government grant until 1892, when the contract, as it had now become, was transferred. In 1908, in consequence of Members being dissatisfied with the reports of debates produced by outside contractors, who were allowed to cut back-benchers' speeches to one-third of their length, the House decided that it would have its own staff of reporters, and that no discrimination should be made between the reporting of Ministers' and Members' speeches. Since 1909 the Official Report has been, as far as is humanly possible, and so far as is compatible with the requirement of comprehensibility, a verbatim record of the proceedings.

Fourteen reporters follow one another in taking turns in the House, sitting above the clock in the front row of the Press Gallery. At the end of each turn a reporter dictates from shorthand notes to a typist. The typescript is then revised and passed for sub-editing to the editorial staff. Increasing use is being made of modern information technology. Members residing in the London area find the daily part waiting for them on the breakfast table. Members are allowed to correct errors of their own or slips of the reporter, but cannot make alterations giving a different turn from the spoken words. These corrections are submitted for the approval of the Editor for the purposes of the bound volume.

The committee stages of most public bills are taken in Standing Committees, whose debates are reported and published in a separate series. In the majority of Standing Committees the debates are reported by transcribing from recorded tape.

The reporting of evidence taken before Select Committees is in the hands of a private firm. Joseph Gurney reported the whole of the proceedings at the trial of Warren Hastings (1788–95) and William Brodie Gurney, his son, was appointed the first official shorthand writer to both Houses of Parliament in 1806. Since that time the senior partner of the firm which he founded has held the appointment.

The State Opening of Parliament

At the opening of Parliament the Queen leaves Buckingham Palace in the Irish State Coach, preceded by State carriages bringing the gentlemen and ladies of the Court, and with an escort of Household Cavalry. The coach proceeds through lines of troops down the Mall and along Whitehall to the House of Lords, where it comes to a halt under the great archway of the Victoria Tower. Here Her Majesty is received by the great Officers of State and escorted up the Royal Staircase, lined by the Household Cavalry, to the Robing Room. Then a procession is formed which passes slowly through the Royal Gallery between lines of Yeomen of the Guard into the Prince's Chamber where the Gentlemen at Arms are on duty. At the head of the procession come pursuivants and heralds, followed by officers of the Court in full dress. The Comptroller and Treasurer of the Household (both generally Members of the Government of the day) carry white wands, the Private Secretary and the Keeper of the Privy Purse follow in their uniforms; after them come the great Officers of State in their robes, the Lord High Chancellor carrying the Purse, the Lord President of the Council, the Lord Great Chamberlain and the Earl Marshal, and two Peers, one holding aloft the gold-sheathed Sword of State, the other the Cap of Maintenance in red velvet, trimmed with ermine. Then comes the Queen, followed by scarlet-clad pages bearing her train. She wears the Imperial State Crown in which among glittering diamonds and pearls are set the ruby which King Henry wore at Agincourt and the sapphire of Edward the Confessor. As Her Majesty enters the House of Lords, the entire assembly rise to their feet. It is a brilliant gathering – tiara'd peeresses in gowns of every hue; peers in their scarlet robes miniver-barred

19 The Queen reads the Speech from the Throne to both Houses
    of Parliament

and gold-fringed; archbishops and bishops; judges in their full-bottomed wigs; and the Diplomatic Corps displaying a galaxy of uniforms and sparkling orders. Then the Queen, being seated on the Throne, bids the company be seated.

At this moment the Lord Great Chamberlain by Her Majesty's command raises his wand, and upon this signal the Gentleman Usher of the Black Rod goes to the House of Commons. When he reaches the door of the House he finds it slammed in his face by the Serjeant at Arms, symbolising the Commons' claim to exclude the Sovereign (and, indeed, any stranger) from their deliberations, the last occasion on which the reigning monarch entered the House was when Charles I came to arrest the Five Members in 1642. He then knocks three times, the door is opened, and he advances up the floor of the House, making three obeisances, and delivers his message commanding the attendance of 'this honourable House' in the House of Peers. Then the Speaker, in State robes, preceded by the Serjeant at Arms bearing the Mace and followed by the Clerk of the House, and the Speaker's Chaplain and Secretary, leads the Members to the House of Lords. The Prime Minister walks with the Leader of the Opposition, and they are followed in order of precedence by the other Ministers and the principal Members of the Opposition in pairs. When the Speaker and the Commons have arrived at the Bar, the Queen, having received a copy of the most Gracious Speech from the kneeling Lord Chancellor, reads it to the assembled Lords and Commons. The Speaker bows and retires, followed by the Members of the House of Commons to their own Chamber, while the Queen leaves the House of Lords, and the glorious pageant disperses.

The ceremonial has changed little in the 400 years since the first Queen Elizabeth opened Parliament. Her speech on 2 April 1571, as reported by Sir Simonds D'Ewes, was brief:

> My right loving Lords, and you our right faithful and obedient subjects, We, in the Name of God, for His Service, and for the safety of this State, are now here assembled, to His glory, I hope; and I pray that it may be to your comfort, and to our common quiet and to yours and to all ours for ever.

The State Opening of Parliament was first televised in 1958; it has been regularly shown since then.

The Maces

House of Lords

The House of Lords uses two maces. The older of these is of the time of Charles II. It is of silver gilt, 5 ft 1 in (1.5 m) long and bears no hallmark. Round the head, in four panels, are a rose and portcullis, a fleur-de-lis, a thistle and a harp, severally crowned and with the cypher of C II R. The other mace is of the time of William III and was made by Francis Garthorne, a silversmith of London. It is also of silver gilt, 5 ft 1¼ in (1.5 m) long and is made up of pieces of more than one mace, the foot-knop being of different work from the rest of the mace. The head bears the initials GR, but the G replaces an earlier W. On the cap of the crown are the Royal Arms.

The House of Lords maces, like the one used in the Commons, are symbols of royal authority and one of them accompanies the Lord Chancellor, both in the House of Lords and elsewhere, when he appears officially and the Sovereign is not present. In the House of Lords the Mace is laid on the Woolsack behind the Lord Chancellor at all times when the House is sitting, except at the State Opening of Parliament when the Sovereign is present in person.

House of Commons

The Mace in the House of Commons was originally the emblem of office of a Royal Serjeant at Arms, but has become the symbol of the power and privileges of the House. It symbolises the authority delegated to the Commons by the Sovereign, who resumes possession of it when Parliament is prorogued. Without it the House cannot be properly constituted. It is carried by the Serjeant at Arms before the Speaker in the procession to prayers, which opens each sitting of the House; it is carried out by the Serjeant when the House rises each night. When the House is constituted with the Speaker (or Deputy Speaker) in the Chair, the Mace lies on two rests on the Table of the House; when the House goes into Committee, the Speaker leaves the Chair and the Serjeant at Arms places the Mace on two supports below the Table. Until a Speaker has been elected the Mace is kept under the Table, and is placed on the Table as soon as the election is over to show that the House is properly constituted for its own proceedings. The Speaker is preceded by the Mace when going up to the House of Lords and on official occasions.

In 1649 the House of Commons ordered a mace to be made at its own expense by Thomas Maundy. This was the mace which Oliver Cromwell bade one of his soldiers remove as that 'Fool's Bauble', on the dispersal of the Long Parliament on 20 April 1653. It was, however, returned. At the Restoration, the House ordered on 21 May 1660 that two new maces be provided forthwith. The present Mace in the Commons has been in use there since the end of George III's reign and is most likely to have been built up from the pieces of two maces made in 1660, with an orb and cross of about 25 years later. The Mace is silver gilt, and measures 4 ft 10½ in (1.4 m) long; its overall weight is 16 lbs (7.2 kg). The shaft consists of one short and two long sections, which are chased throughout with longitudinal branches from which spring roses and thistle flowers. The head is divided into four panels containing respectively a crowned rose, a thistle, a harp and a fleur-de-lis. The whole is surmounted by a royal crown with the orb and cross. On the cap are the Royal Arms with the garter supported by a crowned lion and unicorn, with the motto *Dieu et mon droit* and the initials CR. The Mace is not hallmarked and bears no inscription, date or maker's mark.

The House of Commons has presented maces of various designs to a number of Commonwealth countries.

The Speaker's State Coach

The Speaker's State Coach is the oldest of the three great ceremonial coaches, the other two being the Royal State Coach and the Lord Mayor's Coach. It was designed for William III in 1698 by Daniel Marot, a fugitive

20 The Speaker's State Coach

French Huguenot in Holland, and handed over to the Speaker by Queen Anne. The coach weighs 2¾ tons (2.7 tonnes), is heavily gilded and elaborately carved. The lower panels are painted with emblematic subjects. One door panel has a seated figure of Britannia to whom women are bringing fruits; the offside door panel shows King William seated, with Liberty, Fame and Justice (blindfolded) beside him being presented with two scrolls – one inscribed 'Magna Carta' and the other 'Bill of Rights'. Beneath each door panel are crossed maces surmounted by a cup. The four side panels show figures of Literature, Science, Plenty and Architecture. The back panel probably refers to the coming of William and Mary to England, with a ship in the background, William and Mary on the left and Britannia with a lion on the right. The paintings are by Cipriani. There are no brakes on the coach, and since the speakership of Mr Shaw-Lefevre (1839–57) it has been drawn by dray-horses provided by Messrs. Whitbread & Co., in which firm he was a partner.

The coach is only used for great ceremonies of state. The Speaker is entitled to an escort of one Household Cavalry trooper who rides beside the window of the coach, and two mounted policemen ride before and behind it.

The crests of the speakers who have used the coach are inscribed on the panels. It was used at the presentation of an Address by the House of Commons to Queen Victoria on her Jubilee in 1879, the Coronation of King Edward VII in 1902, the Coronation of King George V in 1911, the Silver Jubilee of King George V in 1935, the Coronation of King George VI in 1937, the Coronation of H.M. Queen Elizabeth II in 1953 and the Silver Jubilee of H.M. The Queen in 1977.

Appendix

The Gifts of the Commonwealth

These gifts were given in 1950 by countries of the Commonwealth to mark the rebuilding of the Chamber of the House of Commons.

ADEN   Members' Writing Room table

AUSTRALIA   Speaker's Chair in Australian black bean

BAHAMAS   Minister's writing desk and chair

BARBADOS   Minister's writing desk and chair

BERMUDA   Two triple silver gilt inkstands

BOTSWANA   One silver gilt ashtray

BRITISH HONDURAS   Minister's writing desk and chair and Royal Coat of Arms

CANADA   Table of the House in Canadian oak

CEYLON   Serjeant at Arms' chair

CYPRUS   Members' Writing Room table

DOMINICA   One silver gilt inkstand

FALKLAND ISLANDS   One silver gilt ashtray

FIJI   One silver gilt inkstand

THE GAMBIA   Two silver gilt ashtrays

GHANA   Minister's writing desk and chair

GIBRALTAR   Two oak table lamps with bronze shades

GRENADA   One silver gilt inkstand

GUERNSEY   Minister's writing desk and three chairs

GUYANA   Four triple silver gilt inkstands

HONG KONG   One triple silver gilt inkstand

INDIA   Entrance doors to Chamber

ISLE OF MAN One silver gilt inkstand and two silver gilt ashtrays for Prime Minister's Conference Room

JAMAICA Bar of the House in bronze

JERSEY Minister's writing desk and chair and silver gilt inkstand

KENYA Minister's writing desk and chair

LEEWARD ISLANDS Six oak table lamps with bronze shades

LESOTHO Two silver gilt ashtrays

MALAWI One triple silver gilt inkstand and one silver gilt ashtray

MALAYA Minister's writing desk and chair

MALTA Three silver gilt ashtrays

MAURITIUS Minister's writing desk and chair

NEWFOUNDLAND Six chairs for Prime Minister's Conference Room

NEW ZEALAND Two dispatch boxes in pururi

NIGERIA Furniture for Aye Division Lobby in iroko

NORTHERN IRELAND Two clocks and division clock for the Chamber

PAKISTAN Entrance doors to Chamber

RHODESIA Two silver gilt inkstands with paper racks

SABAH One table and five chairs for interview room

SEYCHELLES Minister's writing desk and chair

SIERRA LEONE Minister's writing desk and chair

SINGAPORE One table and five chairs for interview room

SOUTH AFRICA Three chairs for Clerks at the Table

ST HELENA One Chairman's chair for Prime Minister's Conference Room

ST LUCIA One silver gilt inkstand

ST VINCENT One silver gilt ashtray

SWAZILAND One silver gilt ashtray

TANGANYIKA One table and five chairs for interview room

TRINIDAD AND TOBAGO Minister's writing desk and chair

UGANDA Furniture for No Division Lobby in mvule

ZAMBIA Two pairs of bronze brackets for the Mace

ZANZIBAR One silver gilt ashtray

Bibliography

Advisory Committee on Works of Art in the House of Commons, *Report*, 1955

Apollo, May 1992 issue

Aslet, Clive, 'The House of Lords Ceiling Restored', *Country Life*, 8 November 1984

Baines, Frederick, *Report on the Condition of the Roof Timber of Westminster Hall*, Cmnd 7436, 1914

Barry, A., *The Life and Works of Sir Charles Barry*, 1867

Biggs-Davison, Sir John, and Chowdharay-Best, George, *A Catholic Companion to the Houses of Parliament*, 1990

Binski, Paul, *The Painted Chamber at Westminster*, 1986

Bond, Maurice, *Historic Parliamentary Documents in the Palace of Westminster*, 1975; *Guide to the Records of Parliament*, 1971 (*A Short Guide*, 1980, is available from the Record Office); ed., *Works of Art in the House of Lords*, 1980

Brayley, E. W., and Britton, J., *The History of the Ancient Palace and late Houses of Parliament at Westminster*, 1836

Clark, Kenneth, *The Gothic Revival*, 1964

Cobb, H. S., ed., *Parliamentary History, Libraries and Records*, 1981

Cocks, Sir Barnett, *Mid-Victorian Masterpiece*, 1977

Colvin, H. M. (general editor), *The History of the King's Works*, 1963–82

Cooke, Sir Robert, *The Palace of Westminster*, 1987

Cooper, Ivy M., 'Westminster Hall' and 'The Meeting-places of Parliament in the Ancient Palace of Westminster', *The Journal of the British Archaeological Association*, 1936 and 1938

Cope, Charles Henry, *Reminiscences of Charles West Cope, R.A.*, 1891

Cormack, Patrick, *Westminster: Palace and Parliament*, 1981

Darwin, John, *The Triumphs of Big Ben*, 1986

Davies, J. M., 'Red and Green', *Journal of the Society of Clerks at the Table in Commonwealth Parliaments*, 1968

Department of the Environment, *Archaeological Investigations in New Palace Yard 1972–74. Interim Account, 1975. Catalogue of the Burning of the Houses of Parliament*, 1984

Harvey, John H., *Henry Yevele*, 1944

Hastings, Maurice, *Parliament House*, 1950; *St Stephen's Chapel and its Place in the Development of the Perpendicular Style in England*, 1955

House of Commons, *Report from the Select Committee on Westminster Hall Restoration*, 1885. *Report from the Select Committee on House of Commons (Rebuilding)*, 1944. Various reports from the Select Committee on House of Commons (Services)

Jones, Christopher, *The Great Palace*, 1983

Mackenzie, Frederick, *The Architectural Antiquities of the Collegiate Chapel of St Stephen*, 1844

Ormond, Richard, *Catalogue of Daniel Maclise 1806–1870*, 1972

Phillips, Alan, *The Story of Big Ben*, revised edition 1976

Pointon, M., *William Dyce 1806–1874*, 1979

Port, M. H. (editor), *The Houses of Parliament*, 1976

Public Information Office, House of Commons, various fact sheets and House of Commons Library Documents

Rogers, Phillis, 'Victory and Disaster: Armada Tapestry', *Country Life*, 6 October 1988

Royal Commission on Historical Monuments (England), *An Inventory of the Historical Monuments in London, Vol. II, West London*, 1925

Ryde, H., *Illustrations of the New Palace of Westminster*, 1st series 1849, 2nd series 1865

Sainty, J. C., 'The Meeting Places of the Houses of Parliament at Westminster', *Journal of the Society of Clerks at the Table in Commonwealth Parliaments*, 1976

Saunders, Hiliary St George, *Westminster Hall*, 1951

Sitwell, Major-General H. D. W., 'Royal Serjeants-at-Arms and the Royal Maces', reprinted from *Archaeologica*, Vol CII, 1969

Smith, J. T., *Antiquities of Westminster*, 1807

Stanton, P., *Pugin*, 1971

Taylor, A. J., *The Jewel Tower*, 1965

Thorne, Lt. Col. P. F., *The Mace in the House of Commons*, 1971; *Ceremonial in the House of Commons*, Revised edition, 1974

Victoria & Albert Museum, Report on *Furniture in the House of Lords*, House of Lords Paper No. 133 (1973–74)

Walker, R. J. B., *A Catalogue of Paintings, Drawings, Sculpture and Engravings in the Palace of Westminster*, 1959 etc., 7 vols. typescript with annual supplements; available for consultation in the House of Lords Record Office

Wedgwood, A., *Catalogues of Pugin Drawings* (i) RIBA, 1977 (ii) Victoria and Albert Museum, 1985

Williams, O. C., 'The Topography of the Old House of Commons', 1953. Not published

Wright, A., and Smith, P., *Parliament Past and Present*, 1903

The Houses of Parliament
Outline Plan of the Principal Floor

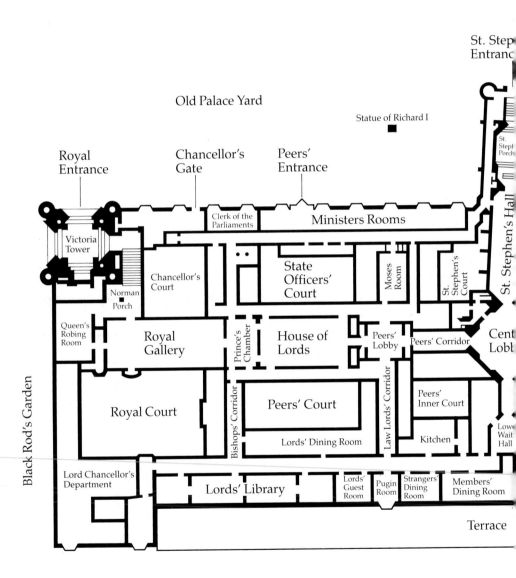

Old Palace Yard

St. Stephe
Entranc

Statue of Richard I

Royal
Entrance

Chancellor's
Gate

Peers'
Entrance

Clerk of the
Parliaments

Ministers Rooms

St.
Steph
Porch

Victoria
Tower

Chancellor's
Court

State
Officers'
Court

Moses
Room

St.
Stephen's
Court

St. Stephen's Hall

Norman
Porch

Queen's
Robing
Room

Royal
Gallery

Prince's
Chamber

House of
Lords

Peers'
Lobby

Peers' Corridor

Cent
Lobb

Royal Court

Bishops' Corridor

Peers' Court

Law Lords' Corridor

Peers'
Inner Court

Black Rod's Garden

Lords' Dining Room

Kitchen

Low
Wait
Hall

Lord Chancellor's
Department

Lords' Library

Lords'
Guest
Room

Pugin
Room

Strangers'
Dining
Room

Members'
Dining Room

Terrace

Index

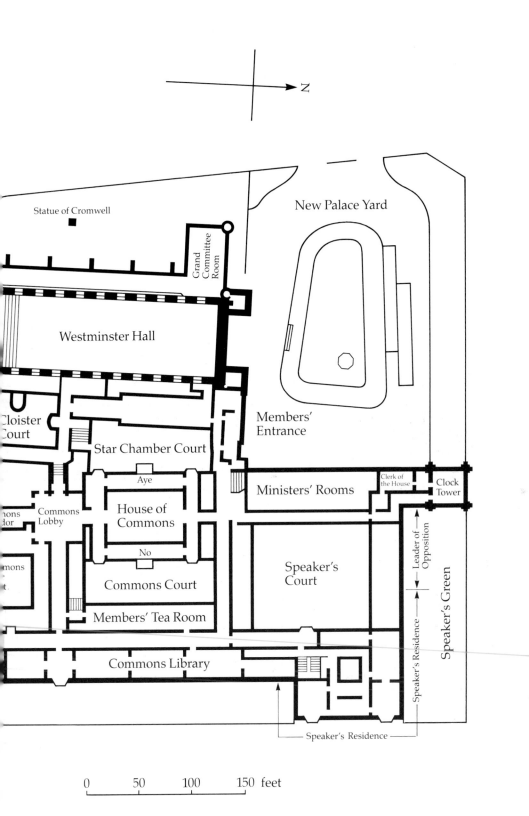

N

Statue of Cromwell

New Palace Yard

Grand Committee Room

Westminster Hall

Cloister Court

Members' Entrance

Star Chamber Court

Aye

Ministers' Rooms

Clerk of the House

Clock Tower

Commons Lobby

House of Commons

No

Speaker's Court

Leader of Opposition

Speaker's Green

Commons Court

Commons Library

Members' Tea Room

Speaker's Residence

Speaker's Residence

0   50   100   150 feet

The Palace of Westminster
at the end of the Eighteenth Century

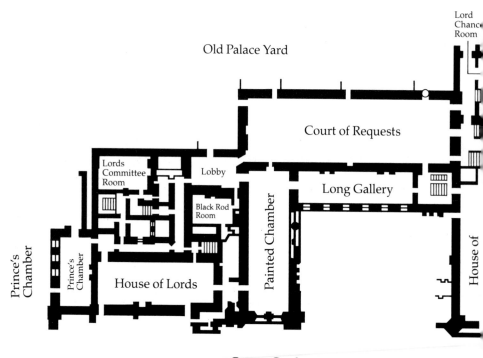

Old Palace Yard

Lord
Chance
Room

Court of Requests

Lords
Committee
Room

Lobby

Long Gallery

Black Rod
Room

Painted Chamber

Prince's
Chamber

Prince's
Chamber

House of Lords

House of

Cotton Garden

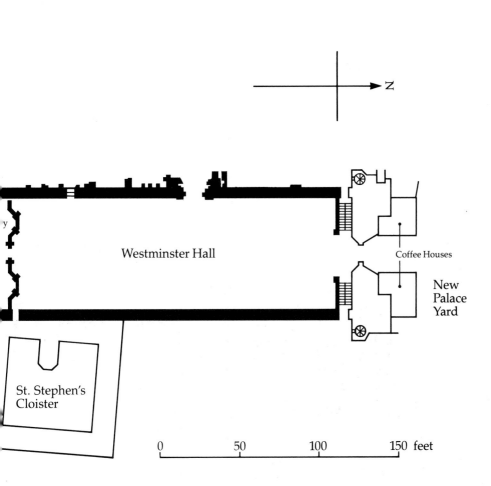

Westminster Hall

Coffee Houses

New
Palace
Yard

St. Stephen's
Cloister

z

0   50   100   150 feet